# PRAISE
## Growing Your S

CW00503243

"Growing Your Separate Ways offers nuggets of deep wisdom and truth to light the way through the confusion and hurt of a breakup. Leah Ruppel will kindly take you by the hand and lead you one step at a time down the pathway of recovery, until before you know it, your heart will feel lighter and your spirit stronger for all you have endured – so that you are ready to move forward with an open, happy and fully healed heart."

KATHERINE WOODWARD THOMAS,
NY TIMES BESTSELLING AUTHOR OF CONSCIOUS UNCOUPLING:
5 STEPS TO LIVING HAPPILY EVEN AFTER.


"This book makes a contribution - "Growing Your Separate Ways" offers a clear process, steps that flow from one to another embracing reflection, evaluation and personal growth. Leah incorporates the essential ingredients into her book to build awareness, helping the reader understand where they are at, whether they want to hear it or not.

Instead of saying 'screw it I am done,' she had a *mindset* going into it and *kindness* going through it."

– JIM SMITH, M.A. RCC, (LEAH'S MARRIAGE COUNSELLOR).

"I put into words what I wanted to find before I knew what it was, as I googled 'amicable separation' and found *Growing Your Separate Ways*. Leah provided a roadmap, a path I could travel. Why re-invent the wheel when I don't have to?"

- JUDITH, READER AND SUPPORTER

# GROWING YOUR SEPARATE WAYS

## BY LEAH RUPPEL

## COPYRIGHT

*Cover Design*: John Matthews

*Interior Design*:  Doreen Hann

*Editing*: Kate Makled & Adrienne Sharpe

Author's Photo Courtesy of John Matthews

# Dedication

*To my children, Chelsea and Jaden, the true loves of my life. The source of my inspiration to make a difference in this world*

# TABLE OF CONTENTS

# INTRODUCTION

"No matter where you are on your journey, that's exactly where you need to be. That next road is always ahead."
**OPRAH WINFREY**

Are you tired of being unhappy, frustrated, unfulfilled, or feeling stuck? Perhaps you are struggling with the choice of staying unhappy or being divorced. See the problem? Your brain associates staying in the relationship and ending it as equally painful. Therefore, no decision is made, resulting in complacency, mediocrity, and a feeling of being *stuck*.

Marriage still remains one of the most important social institutions, yet marriage rates are declining and divorce rates are rising. The traditional picture of a family is being transformed. You could Google statistics on divorce in the world and find alarming percentages of divorce rates across most countries. There may be many contributing factors for this divorce trend such as longer life expectancies, more women working, and less women who are economically dependent on husbands. It is easier to divorce these days, and there appears to be a shift towards self-awareness and independence, perhaps more pronounced in the female population. Many couples are choosing to separate over living in unfulfilling relationships.

We have been taught through generations that divorce is messy and painful. While I am convinced this can be substantiated, I believe that we need to train people to think differently in order to behave differently. There is not enough documented precedence of couples who successfully *un*marry, or at least it doesn't get the same attention as divorce. We need to seek a solution-oriented outcome for life after marriage. We need to evolve a new collective consciousness around the words separation and divorce.

In light of my own personal story, I chose to separate because unhappy wasn't a state I wanted to feel. Reflecting on the stories of many of my clients, I chose to write a book that acknowledges the need for a new consciousness and positive outcomes. Because relationship unhappiness is such a common issue, I want to influence the way couples approach the concept of separation. I feel it's so important to honor the common phenomenon of midlife awareness, it is not a crisis; it is an awakening. Couples need support on their journeys as they move forward toward an outcome where they can thrive separately, not merely survive together.

*Growing Your Separate Ways* is a book about possibility, the potential for a new way to be. I want to share my 8 Progressive Steps, a guide that assists couples to find their own way to grow cohesively and independently. It is time we embraced the possibility of new forms of relationships and new definitions of family. My 8 Progressive Steps are designed to be implemented strategically in order for couples to learn how to respect each other on their own unique journeys–regardless of whether they are growing in love or growing *out* of love.

Marriage is a journey of love, an intention to unite two people to grow together, to build a life, pursue shared dreams and goals, and share trials and tribulations *forever*–or, as many sets of vows are written, *till death do you part*. In reality, two people do not have to be married in the religious or governmental sense to still have the intention to "grow together" in love and life. What happens when that preconceived notion of marriage, of *forever*, begins to wane and the fairy tale is long over? The realization sets in that you are no longer in love? Worse yet, sex has become non-existent. Arguably, more people climb into bed with you now due to the influence of social media. We are more connected to people on social media yet we are more disconnected than ever; we are in an era of attention seekers, where likes are more important than the desire to be loved unconditionally. Add in the stress of finances when it is increasingly more difficult to manage debt load. Some couples begin to experience their "unhappily ever after" as the plan alters from their original intention.

When the "plan" has altered and the intentions around your relationship shift–creating consideration around a whole new way of being together–what do you do? Is it an all-or-nothing question? Is it a question of where your relationship falls on a spectrum of striving for a wonderful marriage versus accepting a debilitating divorce? The cultural conversation around divorce is steeped in negativity and shame. There are enough examples of couples in less than desirable circumstances who choose to avoid the stigma and pain of separation or divorce, but is the cost of staying in a dysfunctional, unsuccessful relationship worth the price of your happiness?

Imagine the possibility in creating a new definition of relationship, the potential for a friendship that celebrates the best of each individual and their contributions. If the journey towards a *separation* held the same intention of love and respect as did the journey towards *becoming one*, the potential for "conscious uncoupling" can exist. I became intrigued with this idea myself when I learned about "conscious uncoupling," a term created by psychotherapist and author Katherine Woodward Thomas.

Recognizing that people *do* grow apart in different directions—and nurturing that growth in choosing a continued friendship—preserves some of the reasons for the original attraction to one another. Being free from the need for blame and shame, and choosing to process the emotional and practical separation as a team, can create a very different experience of *moving on* than what is frequently portrayed in the media. Understand that there is freedom to make choices in all things, to decide that happiness trumps suffering. By choosing to identify what isn't working, and discussing ways to move forward together yet separately, you leave room for possibility; this is essential for growth.

My client Rachel, a 46-year-old woman, had everything going for her, as she explained to me, yet she was so unhappy. She was married to Brent for fourteen years, and her kids ages 13 and 15 attended high school. She had the large house in suburbia, a good-paying job with the government, upstanding teenagers, a wonderful husband, and a large social network, and she was miserable. This feeling she had been experiencing was lingering for years, but she continued to bury it. She told herself stories, like it was because she was stressed from work, or tired from managing the household. It was *normal* to feel like this, at least so it seemed when all her other friends– most of whom were moms in the neighborhood–complained of the same state of being. Whenever she had the opportunity to have coffee with the school moms on a holiday, the room was filled with complaints of what wasn't working in each of the women's lives. There was something that had been nagging her consistently for almost a year with regard to her relationship and sense of connection to her husband. She felt she wasn't in love with Brent anymore, yet the thought of divorcing was not a consideration, so she inevitably felt stuck with these opposing truths. Rachel felt she had no choice but to stay in her marriage because she believed breaking up the family and hurting the kids would be devastating. And besides, she wondered, what would everyone think of her if she were to leave?

It was apparent that Rachel was more concerned about how she would be judged by others, which often paralyzed her from making decisions that were autonomous and directive. She always held a high standard for herself and, continually throughout her life, it was evident that the decisions she made were frequently based on how she would be perceived. When Rachel completed her undergraduate degree in business administration, she immediately got a job working with the government. This opportunity landed her a great position with a decent salary at the age of 22, replete with benefits and a great pension plan. Rachel was the middle child who had long struggled to be acknowledged by her parents. They had high expectations for her and her siblings when it came to academics. Rachel never truly felt supported in her aspirations, as most of the attention was directed towards her siblings. Her mom had been a domestic engineer, taking care of the family and house duties. Rachel's dad owned his own engineering firm, and did a good job of providing for the family. Rachel's perspective on relationships was born out of her parents' blueprint for what marriage meant and their definitions of the roles of husband and wife. From the time Rachel was a little girl, she remembers wanting to be married to a hard-working man, to have a traditional wedding, raise a family, and introduce a career, a slight shift from her mother's role.

Rachel dated several guys throughout university but never met anyone she would consider marrying; after all, she wanted to marry for love. Her ideal seemed so far in the future, her vision of the perfect relationship, of growing together in life and in love. After a string of disappointing relationships, Rachel met Brent who had just been transferred from Calgary to her office. At the age of 30, Rachel was beginning to feel her biological clock ticking and was much more open to having a serious relationship at that point in her life. Something clicked the moment Rachel and Brent met up for their first coffee date; an office romance was brewing. Perhaps it was divine timing, but they quickly grew closer in love, and fast forwarded into an apartment together.

The two were inseparable, living together, working together, travelling, and planning for the future. Rachel's blueprint for her life was unfolding exactly as she had envisioned. She was in love and knew that this was the one she would marry, and she saw herself growing in life beside him.

Fast-forward 16 years, and Rachel goes about her day trying to manage the feeling that there is no way out of this situation. She no longer feels a connection to Brent. Sex has been non-existent for two years; there isn't even the occasional touch. She is stressed out at work, her bottled-up tension carries over into her commutes home, and then inevitably she takes it out on the family as soon as she walks through the door. Rachel and Brent could no longer communicate or share thoughts or feelings on the same level as they once successfully did. They had grown apart over a two-year period, existing in the midst of running the family business, which included keeping up the house and shuffling kids to and from activities. It became a friendship of convenience, roommates, more or less, who occasionally passed each other as they went through the revolving door.

Rachel felt like she had no choice but to endure the struggle, and to stay; the tension inside of her built up continuously to the point that she was beginning to feel physical pain. She felt like the energy was being sucked out of her every time she was in his presence. No one really noticed, not even the kids, because that was the blueprint they were adopting for what was normal. Rachel was tormented in the middle of the night with the thought of disassembling the definition of family they had worked so hard to create. What would they think of Mommy now? Where would everyone live? She couldn't imagine living without her kids every day. She didn't want to be labelled as a single mom, because all her friends said it was so hard. How could she survive on her own financially? Rachel felt there was no way she could make such a bold move...so she reconciled herself with waiting it out.

Here I proclaim, "It doesn't have to be that way!" Rachel had a choice, as do YOU, to have an outcome that is more suitable to how she would prefer to envision her future and her definition of family. Nobody ever wrote a rule-book about how to separate or divorce amicably–and every relationship will be unique. Rachel still wanted a friendship with Brent, but did not want to continue what she felt was the charade of a marriage. It may be the expectation or institutional belief that marriage is forever, but that doesn't mean people *can't* choose something different. The journey of separating in love is a concept that is built out of respect, with a mix of good intention and strategic planning, much like that of marriage. Rewind the fabricated love story and embrace the evolution of yourself and your relationship in order to create a new way of being, a different story.

Taking on a new definition of family, and holding the values that were true for them, Rachel and Brent chose to create a new path that allowed them to continue growing individually, but also together. By communicating their good intentions, sharing their ideals around raising kids, and supporting the family potential going forward, they were able to create possibility where there once was none.

Does any part of Rachel's story resonate with you? Perhaps you are feeling as if there is no more hope for happiness in your life, perhaps you too are feeling stuck in an unhappy loveless marriage or relationship. Maybe you feel trapped because you have become somehow comfortable with the status quo, or still hope for the *happily ever after*. Change is challenging, yes? After all, in some ways succumbing to complacency is better than the alternative story–that of being miserable and alone–so you are faced with a decision of choosing pain or pain. This negative loop can continue if nothing exists to break this pattern. You keep telling yourself things like, *I don't have the confidence, I can't afford to be on my own, I don't know how to get out of this situation, I don't know how to be happy*. These are common excuses, along with all the other beliefs and non-resourceful questions you use to support the belief that you don't have a choice. If you have reached the state of comfortably numb, you have succumbed to the belief that your future happiness is impossible. One of the most powerful attributes of humans is the power to choose. Exercise this power and doors of possibility open and beliefs become redesigned.

Have you ever felt comfortably numb in a relationship? Perhaps this is where you are now, and this book will demonstrate that hope exists and that anything is possible for your future. If you want to create a new reality for you and your family, the definition will look much different than your original one. I am here to say that is ok! You have an opportunity to design your future self and relationships by visualizing what you truly want. It is true – anything is possible, and I want to remind you that you are human, therefore you can exercise choice. There will be times when you question yourself and it does not mean there is something intrinsically wrong; it could just be a calibration for determining what *is* right for you. Formulate better questions and your brain will present resourceful answers to you.

I had a pebble in my shoe, so to speak, an analogic description for the past couple of years of my marriage. This pebble eventually became a rock, impossible to ignore, demanding that I make some decisions to remove it from my shoe (i.e. from my life). I chose to do something about my situation because it was affecting every part of my being. *So, I get you!* I understand how you might feel about not having a choice, at least not yet. My belief is that a mom is the proverbial glue within the family, a maternal matrix of care. You can't imagine not being the captain of the family ship and navigating your intended life plan? This book is filled with stories that you may relate to, either for yourself or someone you know. Excerpts from these pages will touch you, or, in turn, affect a loved one who finds their potential is stifled by some intrinsic or extrinsic factors. Perhaps you or someone you know has a metaphorical pebble in their shoe. This book can be a freedom script, a playbook of independence, a personal manifesto; pages of possibility.

## What is possible for you?

For Rachel and what she envisioned, having her freedom again would help to make everything in her life simpler. Instead of feeling like she was drowning in expectation, she would be able to have something to look forward to in hopes, dreams, and personal agency. Her confidence was shaken because what she once was so sure of–her love for Brent and desire to create a life together–became a dismal daily scenario filled with frustration, sadness, stress, and pain.

Rachel even wondered what it would be like to be in love again. Would she get another shot at it? As she approached 50, she shared some common fears about dating, like, who wants to start over again? Who would be interested in an old lady with *baggage*, a loose term used to describe a divorced woman with kids and a story. Where do all the divorced people go? The unloved, the unworthy, the lost souls? Some hold a belief that separated partners will forever hate each other, with a continual fight over property and custody of the kids. Rachel didn't know of anyone who had divorce stories that were positive. In fact, how often do we hear about the successful break ups? Truth is, Rachel was scared to death. Her kids would have to split homes. What if this caused them to do poorly in school, get into trouble, try drugs to mask their pain and suffering? Kids don't want to tell their friends that their parents are divorcing. She wanted to spare them the shame. Rachel was feeling like a failure just by thinking of all these negative things. That was the biggest realization of her problem—her thought patterns. Her brain was not supporting her with resourcefulness because she was asking the wrong questions and focusing on the problem not a solution. She was so tired, and feeling heavily responsible for the impending destruction of her family that she believed would inevitably happen, if she were to own her truth, and verbalize to her husband and kids what she was feeling.

While this sounds somewhat exaggerated to recount, it demonstrates that Rachel's fear was very real because she had constructed a frightening and desperate image of the dark side of divorce, and supported that reality with evidence of all the worst-case scenarios playing out within her circle of awareness.

# CHAPTER 1

## Who Are You?

"Happiness starts with you – not with your relationships, not with your job, not with your money, but with you."

One of the best ways to disassociate yourself from your situation and to create different constructs of what is possible is to view your relationship as a movie that you are watching. Getting a different perspective of your own or other people's relationships can help support, encourage, and entertain a new way to be. By sharing these select stories of some of my clients, maybe you will find it relatable, causing you to shift your perceptions and beliefs.

Janice is a 50-year-old woman whose two kids are grown, out of the house, with lives of their own. She had been a stay-at-home mom for most of those child-rearing years, and later acquired a part-time job doing floral arrangement to fill her lonely daytime hours. She was in an unhappy marriage, slowly losing the sense of who she was. Her core identity was centered on kids, on being a mom. When her kids moved out, the altered phase of motherhood left her questioning what her purpose was in life. Janice did everything for her kids, and when the intense mothering phase shifted to something much less involved, she felt tension and unhappiness build. Her days were spent cleaning the house, shopping and cooking for the family, despite her husband's frequent absence. When he was home, he rarely spoke to her, and minimally interacted with the kids. Janice had been unhappy in her marriage for about 12 years, yet she felt she had no power to change the situation, and little confidence in her own decision-making. She had relied on her husband for support and practical knowledge most of their married life; how could she possibly make it on her own?

About eight months ago Janice contacted me in desperation, saying she needed to do something about her situation at home, or she would "go crazy." She was taking medication to combat her sleepless nights. She was miserable most of the time, except in the efforts to mask her pain with wine, food, and friends. This served only as a bandaid effect of course, and most often the wine would cause her to feel more depressed about her situation. Janice was carrying unnecessary body weight which caused her to feel worse about herself. Despite her efforts to avoid suffering she was desperate for a change and realized she needed professional help.

The 'crossroads' Janice experienced are surprisingly common for many of my female clients who are in their 40's and 50's; I refer to this phase of life as "mid-life awareness". Awareness opens up the motivations which influence or control our daily lives. Emotions we feel are not the essence of us, our being, they are simply expressions of how we are feeling. Your identity does not need to be overtaken by how you feel.

In my coaching practice, I often will ask some fairly foundational questions of a client in the pursuit of a happier life: "How would you like to feel?" "What would you do if you knew you could not fail?" "If you had 'that' how would that impact your life?" With Janice's conundrum, we initially worked on how she saw herself in the future. To find your true self, you must actually focus on the *possibilities* not the *problems*. Feeling stuck requires a shift in perception from negative to positive energy, allowing one to see the potential for things to be different or better. One of the reasons she felt she was drowning with no way out was she had never imagined what a life without her husband would look like. Her identity was tied into being his wife and her potential for independence was not realized. There is a general sense of finitude of life at this age; clients are struck by a deep awareness that time is running out. Janice said to me, "Who am I?" to which I replied, "You are more!"

We began to do thought work–taking her from a negative frame of mind to one that had more positive intention. She progressed from identifying why she could no longer be in her present situation, to what might happen if she focused on the good and appreciated what was right about it. What we did was break up the negative loop of pain vs. more pain. Instead of being in a negative situation and projecting into a future negative situation, we interrupted her pattern with a strategy of introducing what was possible and good for her. Once she had a vision of what was possible for herself, the rest unfolded organically. Janice was able to construct steps to take with this newfound positive intention for her life. With that shift of perception she was able to transcend from breakdown to build-up. The successful implementation of the 8 Progressive Step process assisted Janice on her journey of self-discovery.

Janice welcomed the shift from breakdown to build-up by simply changing the way she looked at situations. It became clear to her that it was not just the marriage that needed fixing; it was her confidence that had waned over the years. After a few short months of diligent work on herself through weekly sessions, and personal development strategies, she was pleasantly surprised by the strength and positive attitude she had acquired. As Janice's confidence grew she was able to tackle more of the difficult decisions such as moving out on her own. Even though she knew divorce was on her horizon, her perspective had changed. She felt like she had control of her own life and decisions and her intention was to make the process of divorcing less negative. By holding that space of acceptance for herself, her husband, and their relationship, the stress began to dissipate. She was no longer afflicted by the guilt and shame that she had once experienced. Janice was able to reconnect to her authentic self and, as a result, has become more confident and assertive in all her interactions. She has gained a new level of respect from her husband due to the changes in her approach and demeanor. She reported that they were having more enjoyable conversations than at any point in the last decade of their marriage.

The *happily ever after* myth that defines the traditional sense of what marriage should be, seems diametrically opposed to the other side of the spectrum–never marrying, or marriage ending in divorce–that represents failure, singlehood, and something to avoid. I posit that all relationships are on a continuum and all human beings are constantly changing–therefore, it is safe to say that marriage is ever changing, also.

The question that may be most relevant, especially at midlife: Is the relationship changing congruently? Is the united couple growing in alignment? There comes a time, for some people in relationships, that letting each other "grow" should not be viewed as a failure, but as an opportunity to evolve into something much greater. What we assume to be our greatest support could inevitably be our biggest barrier to discovering the potential that exists within us. Knowing the difference and how that is manifested in our relationships is the key.

It seems to be universal within our society to view divorce as a negative. In fact, a great majority of people seem to resort to negativity. It is always a 50/50 choice, and I have always chosen to look at a situation with positive intention and ask, "What is possible for me, for us, and for our new family dynamic?" Divorce rates are increasing; it is time we deconstruct the myth of an all-or-none approach to marriage/relationships and make a conscious collective decision to embrace a new way, a new approach or way of being that honors the relationship, the partners, and kids (if applicable).

Some may argue that it sounds easier in theory than in practice. That could have been true in the case of my client Louise, a high-powered attorney who was married to an alcoholic husband. She was overly stressed and miserable about both her job and her marriage. She did not like the person she had become, and at the age of 49, she had the realization that her life was passing her by. She could not continue to endure this dismal existence. She confirmed that something or someone needed to change before she turned 50. In fact, for Louise, in some ways the conscious management of her life was brought out of hibernation when she had a breast cancer scare at 47. It turned out to be benign, but at the peak of what she felt was a nervous breakdown, she knew that change was inevitable. What she realized in our second session together was that she felt alone most of the time, that her husband was no longer co-creating their life together. The reason she was feeling so dissatisfied with all areas of her life was that she forgot what joy and happiness felt like. She was so dependent on her husband and her staff that she neglected to nurture her own needs. When her husband turned to alcohol and her co-workers turned away, she realized she was a shell of existence. She had lost her *joie de vivre*. As we discovered after the first of the 8 Progressive Steps, she hadn't been aware of the real reason why she was feeling miserable.

Louise had to take the time to work through the process to determine that she was ignoring herself and her needs. She was blaming her husband, ignoring his value despite his addiction, and justifying her story that she constructed about herself and why the relationship wasn't working. Funny thing was, she hadn't discussed it with her husband, friends, or professionals—mostly because she did not want to be shamed and be seen as a failure. After all, she was this high-profile lawyer who ran a successful practice, and how would people react if they only knew the truth? Louise carried this covert persona for a good number of years, convincing herself that she was doing the right thing by staying in the marriage.

However, over time, she felt as if she was being pushed to evolve into something different and with this realization came a rush of fear—and vulnerability. This was Louise's effective point of no return, it was time for self-preservation. She told her husband that she was no longer joining him on his journey to self-destruction and that she needed to take care of herself. She struggled to come to terms with her guilt of leaving her husband after 24 years of marriage, pained by the thought of how her son would judge her for leaving Dad after all these years. As we worked together through time and through each of the 8 Progressive Steps, Louise realized that she still felt love for her husband. However, she felt just as strongly that their journey was definitely growing in separate directions. As she gained clarity, and eventually stood confidently in her vulnerable and transparent truth, Louise realized she wasn't divorcing life and everything she was unhappy about. She was divorcing someone who had shared some really wonderful memories with her in the 24 years together. She began to realize that she could have a life of her own, be happy, and still have a friendship with her husband absent of guilt and blame.

Louise was challenged by the opinions of friends, some of whom had experienced messy divorces. Their advice was harsh and vindictive due to their own memories or circumstances. "Get out, take your money and run," or alternately, "Wait it out because it's not so bad," was the voice of support that she had outside of our proactive coaching sessions. She did originally have a belief that being on her own would be "too hard." She was plagued by the thought of becoming single because her belief was that society seemed to covertly criticize a life lived alone. *There must be something wrong with that person if they aren't with someone.* That is not always the case and I celebrate the examples of people who demonstrate that there *is* something quite right about being on their own.

After a few sessions, Louise had an opportunity to work through years of suffering, unravelling expectations that were handed to her from childhood, to find that voice that had been quietened inside of her. She knew that she could no longer endure the situation she was in and continue to remain silent for fear of judgment. Louise embraced the steps in the process and began her journey towards separation. This time she did so with the intention to remain respectful of her husband, allowing him to be responsible for his life choices. Louise did the necessary work and made the *choice* to get out of her situation because it was making her sick, both physically and mentally. Once she freed herself of the guilt and responsibility of looking after her husband, and her fear of the judgment of others–and put the focus on herself–she was able to see the potential in other areas of her life that she had ignored for too long.

She eventually quit her job as an attorney, and currently does consulting on the side. She volunteers with a troubled youth organization to keep kids off the street. She feels more empowered because she has worked on herself. She is pursuing new interests confidently, because her mental and physical health has improved. She feels more joy at 50 than she has at any other time in her life.

Perhaps you get a sense already that these client examples do have some similarities in that they are getting more in touch with themselves. They are taking notice of what is not working and are aware that they are not as happy as they once were, losing themselves in the shuffle of life. I have a client who is a great representation of a sector of women who are evaluating their marriages and their purposes or place in this world. This is a very broad but common theme in my practice as a professional coach.

Tamara is currently assessing her present relationship, asking herself: "Is this all there is to look forward to?" As it stands, she does not foresee a future with her husband because they really are not on the same page in life. Her challenge is in her belief that her kids are too young to endure separation at this juncture in life, and she is adamant that their well-being is paramount. What is interesting is that her belief must also mean that the well-being of the children is optimized by her being unhappy and staying in a dysfunctional relationship. Here is another example of pain vs. pain, or lose-lose, situation. She will suffer with either decision, so there is no decision to make. Many clients of mine echo the same frustration of having to wait it out until the kids are older.

My first impression was that I was dealing with the common all-or-none perspective of marriage–the happily ever after or failure construct. We have arrived at a time in our history where we can invoke change, we can create a new level of consciousness. That could include a collective agreement about the *possibility* that exists after divorce. The recognition of potential that exists to evolve through a relationship, sharing a dimension of love and respect. Creating a healthy definition of family, and a new concept of living together supporting individual growth, even after separation. That is a healthy and proactive start to erasing the dark and dismal status of divorce. What if we didn't look at divorce as failure and instead saw it as an opportunity? Just by announcing it, a small shift in consciousness and a challenge to our belief system emerges. This is true on an individual and societal plane.

I had a few coaching sessions with Tamara, where initially the goal was to help her get some clarity about who she was, what wasn't working, which was essentially knowing her side of the story. But most importantly, what did she want for herself instead? She was early in the process of gaining awareness that she was wanting to do something to develop herself, maybe take a course or go back to work, but her husband wasn't being supportive of that decision. They were clearly on a different page and Tamara blamed her husband for limiting her. After our coaching conversations, what became apparent was that Tamara was limiting herself. Awareness about what wasn't working, and knowing the specific challenges she was up against, brought her to confront the problem of communication. This is where it fell apart for Tamara and her husband—there was no communication. This seems to be a common occurrence in the breakdown of relationships and business. Communication is the key and as we will explore further in chapter 8, there are many elements of communication for partners that must be exercised in order to optimize the articulation, absorption of information, connection to authentic feelings, and reception of response.

It is important to entertain the chance of rebuilding a relationship, and avoid separation, if a workable solution presents itself in coaching sessions. My 8 Progressive Steps can create that solution at some point in the journey—with the newfound clarity and renewed commitment for both partners—and that is a wonderful outcome. This book was written to touch many lives, not just the ones who are separating. I encourage clients, like Tamara, to exhaust their options of reconciliation before embarking on the path of separation.

Tamara is currently working through the stage of communication, and it is unclear as to the trajectory of her marriage at this time. It is apparent that there is growth happening within each partner and on their relationship as a whole because they have both been doing the required work. It is not easy to work through the process, or to accept the word divorce, admit or accept each other's unhappiness. It is not easy to be visible and open with a partner, exposing vulnerabilities. I cannot overemphasize the point that in order to grow with a partner, together or apart, it is essential to be vulnerable, authentic, respectful–open to the good, bad, and ugly–in the course of renewing or dismantling the togetherness. My 8 Progressive Steps teach you to embrace these values in appreciation and gratitude for the journey you are on.

# CHAPTER 2

## Trust the Process

"It's ok to not have the answer yet. Continue your journey and trust the process."

At this point you may be able to relate to some of these client stories I have shared. Throughout this book, you will learn about an effective process I developed in 8 Progressive Steps that can assist you to navigate possibilities on your journey of personal discovery. I want to let you know that you are *not* alone and for *most* of us, it is this sense of feeling stuck that awakens us to the prospect of awareness. Knowing that you can and *will* find freedom, peace, and happiness throughout your journey because you have a shift in consciousness, or because you create a new definition for yourself. It gives you the resolve and hope to continue.

Perhaps you have been in a rut like this for months or even years. It is ok! This process will work for you whatever stage you are at, and whatever your background circumstances. Nobody needs to feel like they are trapped in a rabbit hole with no way out, with no glimmer of hope. This book gives you the tools to collectively align with your partner on what is possible for you both, as you grow your separate ways. Perhaps you still have dependent children, or will retain ties in a business or within the community. The differentiating element of my process, my journey, and my coaching is that I encourage these roles and relationships to transform, not implode.

Over the past few years I have successfully implemented the 8 Progressive Step strategy with dozens of clients, ensuring successful facilitation, and guidance through the scenarios that have caused them to feel stuck. Hundreds of my female clients have faced common midlife challenges that deal with feelings of loss of self, waiting out their relationships, yet not knowing what they are waiting for, or how to even begin to find themselves again. They feel lost and alone because it is so seldom recognized how common this circumstance has become. It is scary, and perhaps there is even some shame around being in this place, especially when it appears that everyone they know is happy, or pretending to be. This is what we learn in Marriage 101, act like the happy family in public.

The benefit of the 8 Progressive Steps is to provide a repeatable and effective step-by-step process to work through stages of the relationship continuum. This formula meets the core criteria for a successful strategy. This process provides the framework for conscious decision-making. Understanding the options and power to choose those will grow you forward in alignment with your partner, even if you are growing your separate ways.

Here is an overview of the 8 Progressive Steps to support and guide you on your personal journey.

## 1. Awareness – Embrace it!

You *know* something isn't right with the relationship. Are you sweeping things under the carpet and ignoring the elephant in the room? It is time for acknowledgment: owning the good, the bad, and the ugly. Being aware that you are not aligned with your values, the relationship is strained, and suppressed feelings over time have created the comfortably numb phase of your relationship existence. In Janice's case, she was living out her distressing marriage for years, not paying attention to how she was really feeling. She ignored the debilitating effects of this disconnect on her mental and physical health until she could no longer endure the pain.

## 2. Visualization - See it!

How would you *like* things to be? *Who* do you want to be? How will your relationship *look* in the future? What do you *want* for you and your partner and your family? In order to grow forward, you must be able to visualize how you would like to see yourself and your relationship in the future. It is like driving a car, you look further ahead on the road and it feels automatic that your body steers the car straight to the destination. You don't look inside the car or behind you, or at the lines immediately next to you, to get to where you are going. The same is true of effective visualization: if you look ahead, your mind and your actions will be aligned with your vision. If you focus on the stagnant situation you are in, or worse yet, look back where you came from, you will not make any progress in growing forward. Visualization is a powerful tool for success–in love and business.

## 3. Clarification - Understand it!

Detail the specific characteristics of your relationship that aren't working for you. It is important to articulate the areas of your relationship that are strained. What are the behaviors or attitudes your partner has that make you angry? What situations come up that cause the most, or the recurrent, dissention in the relationship? Do you both feel the same way about these things?

## 4. Action - Plan it!

For every characteristic or situation you identified that has negative consequences for you, an action plan is created for resolving each major difference. Nothing happens in life without action–ideally, making a decision and then creating momentum to do something to achieve the outcome you want. Action creates the potential for change. And once you begin taking action, your plan is engaged. Otherwise it is just an idea. It is important to note that any action, even the smallest step in the right direction, can have significant impact on altering your behaviour or your circumstances.

## 5. Communication - Say it!

Too often in life and love, the value of clear, consistent communication gets overlooked as people take each other for granted. We get comfortable in our routines and we assume we know how the other person is feeling, how they think about situations, or what they are going to say before they have uttered a word. Learning to ask questions of your partner, or express conversations that go on inside your head, is a habit and a skill to cultivate. My 8 Progressive Step guide and coaching platform offers exercises in support of improved communication. It is such a vital component in most aspects of human interaction, especially in times of change.

## 6. Knowledge - Own it!

It might take a long time for you to arrive at this stage, even if you think you know a great deal now. After all, I am encouraging you to go on a process of discovery that you may not have done since you were in a very different phase of life. Then I am asking you to try and resolve the differences you have with your partner, and act on them. A good trial and error phase is highly individual, and only you can say definitively when it is exhausted. However, this is the point where you know that all the communication about the characteristics of what is failing in the relationship has taken place, and all the action plans to improve or abolish the pain have been unsuccessful. You stand in your truth and own the decision that you cannot continue to be comfortably numb–or evade the situation any longer.

## 7. Conversation - Have it!

Once you have confidently owned your truth, you must then share it with your partner in a respectful manner. Being completely transparent and vulnerable is the best way to avoid misconceptions, assumptions, and attacks from the receiving end. Sometimes setting ground rules for the discussion is enough. Other times, having some outside help here to guide the conversation is beneficial. Once both partners have accepted the change will happen, the next step is to discuss the situation with the children, family, friends and co-workers, or other stakeholders, in that order *and only if it is deemed necessary*. Conversations are opportunities to bridge the gap of understanding. Proactive communication of the facts helps to avoid conflict and animosity that is created from a lack of information or feeling excluded in some cases.

## 8. Growing forward - Move it!

It is essential to move towards the vision that you created for yourself in Step Two. Momentum is easiest when there is clarity of where you want to go. Focus on that vision of how you want to be and the type of relationship that is possible and the rest falls into place. Perhaps, like some of my clients, the relief and restoration of energy propel them faster than they ever envisioned possible. A lot of energy and emotion are consumed by being stuck and avoiding hard truths, or staying scared and small.

The experience of success at this stage also has some reliance on your follow-through; for example, once the decision to separate is made, the conversation complete, the steps in learning how to separate and establishing a framework to grow individually is paramount.

# CHAPTER 3

## To You, To Me, To Us

"Growing apart doesn't change the fact that for a long time we grew side by side. Our roots will always be tangled, I'm glad for that." ALLY CONDIE

I met the "love of my life" in a philosophy of law class in the final year of my undergraduate degree. I remember how cute it was that he sat beside me in the lecture hall, when only a handful of people were present. He may have been shy, but that was a brave and bold gesture to get my attention. It took three months before we shared our first kiss, a bit of an old-fashioned courtship. We had spent those months studying together and really getting to know one another. To this day, we laugh at his intended declaration of moving on because I didn't seem interested, yet I had no idea that he felt that way. Maybe I was just that young and naïve. After the first kiss, first date, rides in his baby blue Trans Am, and sex between his baby blue satin sheets, we knew that we were totally compatible and we considered a future together. We were both intending to go to law school so we became study partners in preparation for our LSAT tests.

After a year of working with different lawyers, we both, for our own justified reasons, felt the path to law school wasn't really for us. Maybe it was because we were falling in love; I like to think we were actually more in tune with who we really wanted to be, and how we wanted to move forward with our lives.

I turned to my passion and quickly became employed in the health and fitness industry. Derrick pursued his business interests. We had a long courtship of four years. In this time, we travelled and moved in together, while being actively involved in physical fitness. We spent every summer boating in Penticton where he grew up. Derrick came from a Catholic background with strong family values and loving, supportive parents who accepted me as one of their own from the very first meeting.

Derrick had been drafted in his junior hockey days to the Edmonton Oilers, yet did not get to live the dream because of a broken neck he sustained in a game at the age of 16. His passion for playing hockey was sidelined, and for a long time he struggled to find a substitute that matched that passion. I was the city girl born and raised in Vancouver, the only child of two 20-year-old parents.

I had a small extended family with two sets of grandparents who were great role models for marriage, having celebrated 50 years together. My parents had a couple of trial separations in my younger years but they stayed together for my sake and eventually divorced when I was 18. I remember being surprised that they were divorcing because they seemed to be the best of friends, yet they were not in love anymore. They had different interests and plans for their futures that did not include each other. Regardless, I had the best childhood despite the demise of my parents' marriage.

One of the first challenging conversations Derrick and I had was about religion, and how to decide which church we would be married in. I was 25 and he was 28, and we each had strong opinions on what was important to us. Much of our relationship, to this day, has been about compromise and respect for one another's opinions and perspectives. We sometimes agreed to disagree. In this case, we chose the happy medium of Anglican. We definitely took our time having kids and experienced pressure from the family to introduce some grandchildren into the circle. I was focused on my career and my biological clock was not ready to have kids. We were enjoying our lives together, travelling more, cooking together, camping, boating, skiing, and many other adventures. We built our first house together, and moved a couple of times before deciding to start a family. I gave birth to our daughter a week after my 30th birthday; this was the most incredible thing we ever did together. We had spent 8 years together socializing with friends and family but when she arrived, she was the focus and family was the priority. We learned how to be parents together, we shared all the responsibilities of growing a family. We did not have specific jobs or chores, we did everything together and Derrick was and still is one of the most engaged, loving fathers anyone could wish for. I am so grateful I chose him to be the father of my children.

We didn't stop at one kid because I was an only child who always wanted a brother and Derrick had a brother. Two years after the birth of our daughter, we introduced our son into our circle; he completed our perfect little family. Becoming a parent changes you; it isn't all about *you* anymore and all the priorities change. The best interests of the kids becomes the new focus and measuring mark. It continues to be the model that we adhere to in parenting forward.

I turned to my entrepreneurial roots and bought a gym, and Derrick continued to work from our home office, so that we could raise our kids, be active, and present for all their milestones. We were living the "ideal" life with two talented, beautiful children, a big house in a desirable neighborhood, two nice vehicles, a boat, family vacations, and two dogs (one Golden Retriever), which deemed us an "ideal" family. We had goals and aspirations that we continually reached, and we never really settled for typical or average. Our ambitions were to be more successful, be mortgage-free, travel a couple times per year, entertain friends, and drink fine wine. Well, we did most of that, especially the wine part!

Then it hit me... at some point, some 22 years into the relationship, I was becoming increasingly aware of an unsettled, unhappy feeling. I bared my soul in a letter I wrote to Derrick stating that I was tired of sweeping things under the carpet. I feared we were growing apart and perhaps I wasn't "in love" anymore. It was a three-page heartfelt letter that contained all the feelings I had kept inside for a couple years because I didn't want to disrupt what we had built together. It was disappointing to admit we had a problem, and that we really weren't in this ideal space we were pretending to be in. This letter truly represented the elephant in the room that was present, yet neither of us wanted to acknowledge it was happening to us.

This letter was the start of the process of identifying where our relationship was failing. Communication dwindled and we became more fixated on nurturing and supporting our kids—but forgetting to take care of each other. After the letter there were many hours of heartfelt talks where vulnerability and courage were reintroduced back into our conversations, much like in the first four years we were courting. It felt like years since we had connected on that level, and as a result we both agreed that we would go to marriage counselling to learn how to communicate better.

During the period of counselling sessions, we were still dealing with issues about the lack of sex because I was too damn exhausted trying to manage the delicate balance between having a career and being a mom. I took on more things than I was capable of handling, and as a result, I was spending no time on my relationship. I was becoming resentful, too, because my priority was the kids and my needs were not contemplated adequately, so I remember thinking, "Why couldn't he just be supportive and patient and not always have his needs met?" It was a stressful time in my life where I felt I had three children and I was still trying to build a business.

After a couple of years of "trying" with family trips, boating weekends, new bedroom games, I realized that I still had that feeling inside my gut that told me I wasn't in love anymore. I could not see a future together because I was not happy in the place I was in.

In our more final marriage counselling sessions, I found the courage to say out loud, "I am not happy," "I feel as if I need to live separate from you," "I am not in love anymore," and "We are so different, we can't even meet in the middle." Finally, I came out and said, "Life is being sucked out of me." Saying all those things that had been building up in me for so long felt like throwing up. You feel better having it out of your system, but you still feel weak, shaky, and vaguely nauseous afterwards. I didn't know what the next step was, but owning my space and having the courage to admit that it wasn't working was the key step. It was difficult to see Derrick's reaction because the last thing I wanted to do was hurt him or break up our family. I didn't have the answers but I knew that the first step was admitting it and announcing it.

Our counselor thought that we were exceptional clients in that we were intellectually on the same page and had great respect and admiration for each other, yet he had to articulate my message to Derrick in a way that he could receive it. We needed a mediator to help massage the meaning behind the words, so they did not get distorted into something ugly. These sessions always left us with a mix of emotions before, during, and after. It is easy to be on the defensive when you feel someone is criticizing and attacking. It was a long process to try to get my message across that it wasn't about who Derrick was, or why he wasn't the husband I needed, but it was more about the process of growing in different directions.

We were evolving as individuals, and letting go of some old beliefs about our relationship took time, it took years. One thing we can know for sure is that change is inevitable, and while we as individuals are becoming different versions of ourselves, the relationship evolves and takes on new dimensions. All this can be positive growth–*if* the partners are aligned.

During this time, I also remember two things about the timing of the term "conscious uncoupling" which referred to Gwyneth Paltrow's marriage break-up, and how they had decided to consciously continue to be loving parents to their child, forming a new definition of family that worked for them. It hit me like, "That's it! That is exactly what I feel!" What a great concept, and I believed it had been in my subconscious during that five-year journey to separation.

I do also remember the "Fifty Shades of Grey" trilogy came out and I read every one. I remember being in Las Vegas for my daughter's dance convention and there were a handful of middle-aged dance mom friends who were buried in a copy of the book. What a scene that was! One night I was reading the second book in bed and my husband got in his side of the bed and said, "hey why don't you bring your book over to this side?" and I replied, "Don't ruin the moment, that side is reality, and this side is fantasy." I clearly had already distanced myself emotionally from him for quite some time and sex without emotion isn't something I wanted to share with him. So I buried myself in the fantasy of what it would be like to be the character Anastasia.

That was just creating more build up and frustration that I had no outlet for so when the books were done, reality set in and once again we were going through the motions of being a married couple.

We always made a good team, and despite disagreements, we always put our kids first. What kind of wife and mother would I be to break up the family during a challenging time such as his emergency back surgery? I had to adapt and understand that this was only temporary, and there were more important matters that needed attention for the time being. In the meantime, I was stressed out with the workload I had to manage. I was balancing work and kids and home maintenance while Derrick continued to make daily efforts to get back to health.

I quickly noticed that I was focusing on all the things that weren't working and that my thoughts were on why I was unhappy instead of thinking how I could be happier. Our relationship was becoming strained, most of all because we were past the point of no return, I was out of the relationship already. I knew I didn't want to make the process ugly, I wanted to avoid the disastrous stories of our circle of friends who had tumultuous relationships, with affairs, emotional abuse, deadbeat dads, or alcohol abuse. We weren't like that, and I wanted something different for us. I didn't want to be married anymore, but somehow I still couldn't use the word *divorce* because it seemed so final... and negative.

My husband wasn't an asshole, he is a wonderful human being who I still care for. I needed to be straight up front about my intentions to create a new definition of family and a continued friendship born out of love and respect for each other. The kind that we carried throughout our 27-year history together. I have always held a vision of how it would look for us. It isn't the same as the one I held for the first twenty years, but it is still a close version of it. I see us celebrating the weddings of our kids and births of our grandchildren, and all the other little milestones in between. After my parents divorced, they were present at all family traditional celebrations, it was just how close our family was, and an example of how important the value of family tradition was and still is for us.

While Derrick was doing rehab and trying to work through emotional and physical challenges, we remained friendly and continued to share the responsibilities around the house and with the kids. We did spend less and less time in the house together and unless it was a gathering time for dinner before everyone went their separate ways, we avoided time with just us. It was inevitable that the timing to separate was upon us; but starting that conversation always seemed difficult, because it would bring up "our stories" and some of the rehashed subjects that we had already talked about repeatedly. This has always been one of my greatest contentions: to revisit a conversation or situation that has already been discussed and settled, even if not agreeably. I would get frustrated instantly and shut down and leave the room because it was a trigger of anger for me, an example of what was still not working. Communication was beginning to strain and each of us was getting a little short with the other. That is when I knew that I was not willing to ruin the 27 years of good memories and we needed to talk to the kids.

I think I dreaded talking to the kids more than I originally dreaded talking to Derrick, because the kids had no idea of what was going on. Nobody had any idea because we always seemed to be normal and happy when others were around. I agreed that I would do the talking, tell them the truth and that it was me who wanted out of the relationship of marriage. We gathered together in our living room and lovingly told them that our paths were growing in separate ways, and that I no longer wanted to be married. The conversation focused on how we would grow forward as a family and that they would still be our first priority. We would continue to be parents on the same page with their best interests at the forefront. It is so much easier to get to a solution when your best intentions are in place and decisions are made with love and respect for the other person. Timing is important; it may be different for everyone but at the point when you "know" there is no other way to stay and make things work out, then you can begin your own journey with a new vision of independence. Soon after speaking with the kids, the ball was rolling, the real estate sign went up, and separation was a reality. On an emotional level, it was difficult to still kind of be together when we clearly were not going in that direction. So we sold the house, split our assets, and moved into separate residences.

With the intention to remain as friends having respect for each other as parents to our kids, shared custody and the division of property and household items became easy. I realized more than ever that it is just stuff and the most important parts of the equation are the family members and the relationships.

It has only been a few months since all of this has been finalized, but I can say that I feel calmer, and I know that I made the right decision because the tension disappeared, no more tightness in my head and stomach. Living in each other's space, knowing that we were not going to stay together, can be a strain on any relationship. We have gone through the process thoroughly, and our journey to divorce is still unknown, yet we continue to work through the obstacles that present themselves as a learning curve. We arrive with positive intention and support the success and happiness of each other. We continue to set an example for our children so that they can be part of the journey with us. We are creating a new definition of family and nurturing our friendship because we have a history to be proud of.

I want others to know that it *is possible* to grow in separate ways but with the intention to do so with love and respect, the integral part of "growing together" in the beginning. I know that it isn't a great feeling to hold anger and animosity toward the person you once loved. It doesn't feel good and it doesn't align with the core values one may have regarding relationships and family. I want the future generations, our kids, to have better examples of how divorce can be gentle and not leave a trail of destruction behind it.

Our exes will always be our kids' other parents, so it is the right thing to do–to honor your ex and treat them as a human being, not as an enemy. I want to offer hope to anyone who sees nothing, who feels stuck with no way out. I want for everyone who approaches this path to realize there is life after divorce and that continued friendship with new definitions of family is possible. The process of the 8 Progressive Steps systematically works through the transitions of breaking down the marriage to separation with a whole lotta love and learning in between. What an optimal process for personal growth and development.

# CHAPTER 4

## Awareness - Embrace it!

"I find it fascinating that most people plan their vacations with better care than they do their lives. Perhaps that is because escape is easier than change." **JIM ROHN**

Awareness is essentially the beginning of the 8 Progressive Step journey—the stage of initiation, when you become aware that something has changed within the relationship and that it has affected you in some way. The question then becomes one of the depth of awareness: is it about the dysfunction of the relationship factors, or is it deeply rooted in one's self? Generally speaking, it isn't hard to identify that something isn't quite right between two people, but the causes of the challenges are not always specific.

Awareness is the ability to clarify the feelings, thoughts, and behaviors that you experience in certain situations; it is really about noticing these facts. Awareness can also be defined as a form of insight beyond notice, which really delves into the truth about these facts—the deeper knowing about what the feelings, thoughts, and behaviors mean in a situation. Noting any physiological changes, internal dialogue and how it impacts you, is the first step in acknowledging there is a relationship or personal challenge requiring attention.

Awareness includes an understanding of all incidences that may have previously triggered a reaction and became more pronounced due to the repetitive nature of the behavior.

In a Neuro-Linguistic Programming (NLP) session, I find it helpful to take a client back to a triggering emotional situation that caused notable psychological and physiological responses, and explore the reactions those triggers elicited. For example, I have a client named Sophia who came to me for relationship coaching; she didn't know if she and her husband could work things out because they always fought. She couldn't really pinpoint the exact reason why they were not getting along or when she noticed the changes. I asked her, "Sophia, what can you tell me about the way your husband used to talk to you in the beginning of the relationship?" She replied, "Well, he used to look at me when he spoke and would always make time for me when he got home from work." This was a daily ritual for the first three years of their relationship.

Things began to change when her husband Geoff got a promotion and he was often held up late at work. His schedule became busier and he always seemed to be in a rush. So I asked, "What changed at this point, Sophia, what was different about your relationship?" "We stopped talking after work and there was less eye contact, in fact he would rarely look at me." Her expression seemed so withdrawn and sad. I proceeded to ask, "How is his behavior making you feel?" She responded by saying she felt he *didn't love her anymore*. Love is a basic human need as well as shelter, food, and safety; for Sophia it appeared that those needs had been supported by Geoff. Her foundational strength was being questioned and the uncertainty was creating a fear in her. Building awareness around her feelings and calibrating her responses to what she was seeing, hearing, and feeling made it easier to detect some of the underlying issues with her situation.

What was surprising to her was the realization that the small little habits Geoff displayed satisfied the connection she needed to confirm she was the only one, that she was loved. When we really got to the heart of the matter, it turned out that Sophia was concerned that he may have been having an affair–because why else would he come home late and not pay attention to her? To create more awareness for Sophia, I asked more questions about how she arrived at this conclusion.

Our coaching time together was a safe haven for Sophia to explore her own feelings around confidence and self-esteem. At this stage, it was clear to me that she needed to focus on herself first, because she was overwhelmed with the status of their relationship. If the unresolved feelings were left unattended their relationship challenges could have escalated to something more complicated and unnecessary. This scenario is a good example of how *awareness about the facts* of a situation can be different from the *insight of the truth* that exists about the situation. Sophia gained more awareness about her relationship by becoming more aware of the truth inside of her. The real issue was her lack of self-esteem and her perception of how her husband demonstrated love. Too often, we transpose a meaning onto an action that is then falsely corroborated by our own definitions, without asking for clarification from our partner or seeking to understand.

Think of when your partner or child does something that gets a rise out of you. They do it all the time and it annoys you, causing you to react in a way you may not be proud of. Maybe there is more than one thing, but for purposes of simplicity in this exercise, let's just choose one thing. Now if you could identify the *one thing* that is the trigger for you, write that down. Does it matter who is doing this, and does it matter where it happens? Describe what you notice when that trigger presents itself. For example, do you get angry, get defensive, flushed, and quiet? Does it escalate each time the person does it? Is it bringing back memories of the past, or the last time you had it happen? What would happen if you did nothing about this trigger–and it persisted and continued to build inside of you for the next two years? How would that affect you? Try the exercise in the next chapter to alleviate the effect that trigger has on you. If you get stuck on this one and need some assistance email me at straightupcoaching@gmail.com.

# CHAPTER 5

## Visualization - See it!

"A vision is not just a picture of what could be, it is an appeal to our better selves, a call to become something more." ROSABETH MOSS CANTER

Our brain works in pictures; images of good, bad, or ugly can circulate in our minds and follow us throughout life reminding us of an event we would love to reminisce about or one that we beg to forget. Images in our mind elicit feelings in our bodies, it is a powerful strategy to recreate a moment in time as if you were experiencing it again. We want to use visualization in this process for the purposes of creating a new vision of relationship and family dynamics, one absent of negativity.

Visualization can be a powerful tool in shifting our perceptions based on images that we create in our minds. There are many ways people can engage with the power of visualization, such as through meditation, a guided imagery exercise, or even a structured future walk through an ideal scenario.

Visualization exercises in this process help to form a strategy to grow in a positive direction toward the ideal image. It is a glimpse into the future, imagining how you would like it to be. The key to any of the techniques in visualization is to subtract any of the unwanted thoughts and behaviors, so that you are able to experience the feeling as if you were really there. If you had the ability to wave a magic wand, what would your future look like? This is a powerful exercise to move people past their present feelings of being stuck, giving the client control over their possibilities in their future just by imagining it.

Let's give this a try and see what comes up for you. Find a comfortable place to sit or lie down, close your eyes and relax all the muscles in your body. Take a couple of long deep breaths, expelling all the old air containing beliefs you no longer wish to hold. Breathe in all the air that carries possibility within it, and imagine opening your very pores to that possibility around you. Now in this relaxed state, I want you to visualize a time in your life when you were most in love. When you are fully immersed in this vision of being in love, I want you to make that vision brighter and notice how you are feeling. Where do you feel that in your body? What do you notice about your breathing now? Are there any colors surrounding this image? Do you notice any sounds? Take your time and breathe in all the experience of being in love. Now I want you to recognize all the sensations and sights that are available to you with this vision, and I want you to know that you can call upon these at any time you desire to revisit this imagery. I would like you to slowly gather your thoughts and bring them into this present moment and be aware that you have just experienced the power of visualization. How do you feel?

The brain is dominant in visualization or images, and has an incredible ability to recall senses like color, sound, and smell as if you are actually experiencing the situation. Visualization is used at this stage of the 8 Progressive Step journey as a strategy to help you powerfully glimpse into the future of possibility and hope.

I have a great example of how this worked with a client named Lorraine. She came in on her second session complaining about how she was fed up with her husband's smoking because he was so grossly overweight. This extra weight caused him to snore, so she could never sleep; as a result, she was tired all the time. She felt if she didn't get some sleep then she would potentially lose her job because she couldn't focus during the day. She blamed her situation on his behavior, she blamed him for everything that wasn't working in her life. Truth be told, there was so much more going on with Lorraine than the superficial annoyance of her husband's snoring. It was more about the blame and the finger pointing as to why she wasn't happy at home and why work wasn't as productive as it could be. Lorraine was a chronic complainer; she did not take responsibility for most of the things that weren't working in her life. She told me of all the extrinsic factors that made it impossible for her to live the kind of life she wanted for herself. Bingo! This was the perfect lead-in to a visualization exercise for Lorraine.

After a 30-minute guided imagery exercise with Lorraine, she was calmer and more reflective toward her situation and her "overboard" reaction to her husband's snoring. She described, "I realize it isn't about his snoring or his weight gain, it isn't about him at all...it is about me! He is working on a weight loss program and I am not doing anything." She had a vision of herself as 30 pounds lighter and so much happier. She was blaming her husband's snoring for keeping her up at night, which was in turn causing her to be tired at work and not have the energy to exercise. She needed to get out of her state of blaming and take ownership of her present state of health. Through the visualization, she was able to construct some steps that she could take to get to that desired state. Lorraine made some resourceful decisions that aligned with the image of who she wanted to be and decided to take the first step by spending a couple of weeks in the spare room to catch up on sleep. Restful sleep meant productive days, which turned into better health, shared celebrations of weight loss, and the eradication of blame.

Whenever you wish to be on vacation, or you need to take a break from the stress and strain of an overwhelming day, remember the easy self-visualization practice. Find a comfortable, quiet place and close your eyes, imagining a time you were_____ or felt _____. (Fill in the blanks with your own desired feeling states.)

Take a deep breath, exhale, and immerse yourself in that vision. Feel it, notice what is around you, sounds, what do you see, what colors stand out. Who is gathered around you? Is there anyone else there with you? Are there any voices coming from anywhere? Any music playing? Really pay attention to how you are feeling in this state as the visual image remains. Is it a still picture or a movie? Are you watching it as on a screen, or are you an actor in the vision?

What do you notice about your body language? The ability to escape from reality and step inside a place of possibility is a powerful step to creating a compelling future and a new way of being. What is possible for you? If you are interested in being coached through a guided visualization exercise to see how powerful it is for you, email me at straightupcoaching@gmail.com.

# CHAPTER 6

## Clarification - Understand It!

"True clarity and purpose emerge when we see ourselves as we truly are." ELEESHA

What is important to this step of the process is clarifying the characteristics and behaviors that are the causes of the general feeling of unhappiness. You may feel as if the whole situation is negative and you just feel miserable in the relationship–and it transfers over to other areas of your life. What is essential now is to determine what makes you angry, sad, frustrated? More often than not, people are aware that they aren't feeling good, but they don't really know *why*.

When someone asks, "How are you?" the answer may be, "I'm ok," yet the internal dialogue for you is that you are really pissed off because your husband didn't clean up the kitchen last night, you worked late, and then you had no help this morning getting the kids off to school. You have a sense as if you are a solo show and you are required to do everything. That is the general story of why you are just ok, however the specific feelings you refrain from sharing are your anger and frustration.

Imagine the connection and conversations that are possible if someone said, "Good morning, how are you?" Then you responded, "I am so angry I could spit!" This should elicit a response in the greeter such as to inquire, "Why is that?" Trouble is, nobody seems to be that engaged these days; no one wants to listen to our challenges, including our spouses. We are missing genuine support in our daily lives. Forced smiles on our faces and closed body language mask the real feelings we are experiencing buried beneath protective layers of BS.

Getting very specific about sourcing out the exact feeling states associated with the elicited body language is the key to learning the strategies that can uncover the hidden truths.

I have this wonderful client Darla, 45 years old, who initially came to see me because she was feeling like no matter what she did, it wasn't good enough. According to Darla, her husband never appreciated anything she did, her kids never even said *thank you*. In general, she was feeling as if all her efforts were going unnoticed, leaving her to question what her purpose was for working so hard to please everyone. She felt taken for granted, and her body language indicated that she was heavily burdened as she carried the appearance of having the life drained out of her body.

Darla was an active stay-at-home mom of four school-aged kids, and she found herself spending the majority of her day in the kitchen preparing meals and cleaning up. Darla prepares breakfasts and lunches for her whole family, including her husband, because that is "her job." Darla explained to me, "After everyone leaves in the morning and I am left with the aftermath, I just want to run away. It is the same thing every morning, every day, every week and I feel like my family doesn't appreciate the amount of work I do to keep this family running smoothly." So I asked Darla about this generalized feeling of running away, "Can you be more specific about how you are feeling?" "I feel *resentment* that my husband is able to leave and go do a job that he enjoys and not have to do anything around the house. I feel *unappreciated* because I rarely get acknowledged for the efforts I make to keep my family happy and healthy. I am *sad* because I know there's more to life than this and I am missing out!" It was the hamster on the wheel analogy with no means to have it stop, she didn't know how. She felt *guilty* for having these feelings, because she should feel wonderful; a healthy family, a big house, and plenty of family income to enjoy the finer things in life. Frustration was mounting because she didn't know how to make the changes necessary to start living life to the fullest. How could she learn to appreciate what she did have? How could she know that she had everything inside of her necessary to feel better about herself and her circumstances?

By taking her morning scenario of the family ritual, we were able to itemize each of the feelings Darla experienced: resentment, lack of appreciation, sadness, and guilt. We got clarity on what triggered those feelings and how that was being manifested in her demeanor or body language. When we broke down the pool of generalized feelings, she began to notice that there really was only one major thing that was missing. In our few sessions together, she was able to articulate that what she needed most was an opportunity to be heard, someone to listen. A conversation that may involve asking how her day was, or how she was feeling. She also realized that she needed her husband to demonstrate that he cared for her, being attentive to her feelings. When she had the opportunity to talk to her husband and share all the things she had discovered in her "clarification" sessions, she felt reconnected to her husband and felt appreciated once again.

In order to grow forward in the process, you must have clarity on the challenges that exist for you. General dissatisfaction or a blanket of complaints can harness the weight of the world and make the pressures feel truly insurmountable and not move you forward at all, however breaking down the specific feelings that make up the heaviness can elicit immediate strategies for change. It is common for couples to have general arguments about a blend of subjects until nobody is clear what the argument is centered on anymore. Being clear about your points of contention, clarity on the importance of a discussion, as in a business meeting, leads to a path of resolution.

Think about some specific feelings or points you might be experiencing now. Does the reverse of these contentious points satisfy the vision you have of an amicable solution or result? I would like you to write down these points as clearly as you can, even in bullet form, as that is useful to keep it simple. If you can write down the specific and actionable issues, then it is easier to strategize on each of these as we go through the next step in the process.

# CHAPTER 7

## Action - Plan It!

"Action may not always bring happiness; but there is no happiness without action." BENJAMIN DISRAELI

Once you have written down actionable issues and points of contention in your relationship, then we can create a plan to have you move away from those frustrating *stuck* states and create a more desirable place to be. Nothing happens if there is no action, and this is evident with most things in life. Success is built on momentum, forward progression, the act of doing something to elicit a reaction and result. In my coaching business, this is a major contributor to the success of my clients, whether it is related to physical fitness, mental health, relationships, or business. I emphasize the *action planning* strategy with most of my personal training clients. Once you have a goal or an objective, visualize how you would like to see yourself. Get clarity about what that *means* for you. *Prepare* to do the work required to get the result.

What is important to remember and understand about this stage is that the action has to be broken down into smaller steps. For example, it isn't wise to decide to run a marathon next month by taking action to run 10km every day as a training platform. There has to be reasonableness when a plan of action is set in place. There needs to be a clear objective and a measurable result before the plan can realistically be implemented. Most importantly, there needs to be "buy in," meaning you must know why you are taking action. This may be your own buy in, or that of your partner. Ask yourself, "What must happen as a result of me making the effort?," "Why is this important to me?," and "What is the cost of me not doing this action?" These questions create the motivation to inspire action. There is always a continuum in some respect with action steps; there is a starting point (wherever you are is ok), and there is an end point, which represents the goal or the vision of what you aspire to be, do, or have.

Action plans need to be written down to be most effective. There is no glory in an incomplete action plan is there? No satisfaction in weak intention or poor follow through. I am able to easily review someone's progress and make changes to the plan as their intentions are crossed off. In short, the action plan is possible once someone has made the decision that they will not accept certain situations or behaviors any longer, that something must be done to rectify the dissatisfaction. Intense desire built out of immense pain.

Barb was a 41-year-old triathlete who came to me in part because her marriage was strained. She had two core issues to tackle: one, she wanted to fix her relationship; two, she wanted to be number one in her age category in the next triathlon she entered, having only three months to train. After listening to her story, I realized that the two issues really were in direct conflict with one another. She was an incredibly action-oriented woman when it came to training, yet there was a lot of inaction when it came to her relationship. Barb was a competitive athlete and the next triathlon was a qualifier to get into the Kona Ironman, one of the most difficult races to compete in.

This Ironman represented a lifelong dream of hers, and she couldn't understand why her husband was not supporting her aspiration, especially now that it was finally in reach. Her commitment to her athletic achievement was evident. Barb was a type A business owner of a hair salon, with a flexible schedule and a four-hour daily training protocol. She would get out of bed before her husband woke up and hit the local pool for laps. Then when she got home, her husband had already gone to work. They didn't have kids, nor did they plan to because she loved her life as it was. She would head into her shop and check in with the staff, do a couple of appointments herself and then take a lunch break. Having taken her workout clothes with her, Barb could also then go for a quick 10km run, shower at work, take a few more clients before calling it quits for the day. She would generally go home and prep a healthy dinner for her and her husband. But then very often, she would eat first, because she was hungry all the time from the training– and her husband didn't get home till around 6:30 or 7pm. Barb wanted to eat early enough to settle her stomach so she could go to her yoga class either at 6:30 or 7:30. Either way, Barb and her husband rarely ate together; if they did, it was rushed with no time to talk about their days. If Barb did her class at the later time, she would get home, have a shower, put on some pj's, grab a book and a cup of tea, and relax before calling it a night. Sometimes they would read together. More often than not, her husband would be on the computer doing his work or watching television to unwind from his day.

Can you see the issue with their relationship? No communication for sure, but zero time was made available–by either partner–for that to happen. Barb was unhappy with her relationship, yet she was also 'married' to her training and spending most of her hours prepping for her goal, which left no time to work on the vision of the relationship she hoped to have with her husband. In dealing with the case of Barb, I separated the relationship from the triathlon. She was really clear about her goals for the triathlon and what needed to happen; it was her priority in her schedule. Based on her desire to stop the arguing and improve the communication, the relationship needed to be the priority and the focus of *our sessions*. Barb did say that she wanted to have connection with her husband of six years, much like they once did, but she didn't "have the time."

This situation called for an action plan. To begin, we explored with the very first of the 8 Straight Steps to help her gain awareness of the fact that it wasn't that she didn't *have* the time to connect with her husband, she wasn't *making* it a priority in her schedule to book in quality time with him. It is important to distinguish the difference when someone says they don't have time. Once she became aware that her marriage was important to her, and the value of love and companionship was an important value, she understood the necessity of making the effort she had neglected to make for the past two years. She was so self-absorbed in prioritizing her training and commitment to reaching her goal, that she hadn't noticed that attention was not being invested in the areas that mattered most.

The action plan for Barb started with a scheduled session of "couple time" built into her already highly managed work/training schedule. Where there once was no time, now became two hours of quality time together. They even have one day on the weekends that is strictly *their* day; they incorporate something active, in addition to developing opportunities to try new things.

Is there something you have been failing to take action on in your own life? Perhaps you want to lose some weight to feel better about yourself, or increase your self-confidence. Maybe that will benefit you in your relationship or in your work environment. Choose something that you have already clarified you want a *different* result with. Now, visualize how you will feel after having that result; be very specific about the image.

What do you notice? How do you feel? While you are in the desired state, decide on one step you can act on right now to move towards that vision. You may be excited and come up with many steps because your brain is in such a resourceful state. For simplicity, choose only one and write it down.

Let's expand on that action item and make it more like a plan, with some additional information. If your goal was to lose 10 pounds, and you imagined yourself in a new cocktail dress at a work function, everyone was commenting on how good you looked. How did that feel? Hold that vision and feeling for a little longer, it is very powerful imagery and tends to elicit action steps to get more of it. We all want more of a good thing yes?! In that state, you might write down *Run for 20 minutes per day*. Indirectly, the running will help to lose the 10 pounds that allowed you to look amazing in that dress. Running for 20 minutes is the action item, and developing the plan further would be to fill in the blanks such as....*I will run 20 minutes per day at 6 am. I will set my alarm for 5:30 every morning. I will put my running shoes beside my bed. I will ask my girlfriend the night before to meet me at a location*. Perfect... the action plan is set, and it tells you simply what *needs* to happen to achieve your result. No more need to think about it, and no more default. The power of this conscious action trumps the unconscious plan to reach the self-confidence through training and reaching physical goals.

For Barb, she was able to see that once she consciously made the action plan to schedule more quality time with her husband, because it was also a priority, she was able to override the unconscious predisposition to train, since she was seeking the same outcome–self-confidence. Once Barb had taken some action steps on her relationship, she was able to communicate in a civil manner with her husband because they were finally on the same page.

# CHAPTER 8

## Communication - Say it!

"To effectively communicate we must realize that we are all different in the way we perceive the world and use this understanding as a guide to our communication with others." **TONY ROBBINS**

Entire books are written about the art of communication, and, as the quote from Tony Robbins points out, there is an acquired skill to determining how we communicate with someone based on our learned appreciation of differing perceptions. When we have two people in a relationship with opposing models of the world, it is challenging to communicate on the same plane, or sometimes to just simply appreciate where the other is coming from.

What is most challenging about this stage in the process of the 8 Progressive Steps is that often communication intent can be inferred solely from non-verbal cues such as gestures or body language. This can be exceptionally challenging in a struggling relationship, where verbal communication may be nonexistent. How often have you been in a situation where there is some sweeping judgment or inference made from body language, because you have seen it repeatedly and so you or someone else will declare *full knowledge* of what it means? Maybe not, at least not so precisely.

There are many dimensions to this step of the process, but the critical components of communication are:

- set good intentions

- verbalize

- listen

- reciprocate

- honor

Communication is an important skill to practice for success in most areas of life; it is my belief that a majority of issues between people are caused by a lack of communication or some miscommunication. This book will help you to improve your standards of communication, and set clear intention and respect towards your partner, even in the midst of a separation. This fifth of the 8 Progressive Steps, as with all the previous steps, can easily map over to areas of your life outside of your primary relationship. For the purposes of supporting people who want to grow into their authentic selves, we will focus our attention in this chapter on the communication between partners who are struggling in their primary relationships including marriage.

Again, the art of communication is a skill, it is learned from an early age and influenced and developed throughout our lives. There isn't a one-size-fits-all model, so trying to determine valuable, effective communication components is challenging at best. Everyone wants to be heard, get their point across, or have their opinions heard, but the most important ingredient in communication is actually active listening skills.

The art of communication is exemplified when there is an even "flow" in the exchange of dialogue between two people. Our earliest teachings of communication are from caregivers, so we model the communication skills we observed in our most impressionable years from our parents. What is the outcome of poor role modeling of communication in life and love? Unfortunately, there is no formal class curriculum in elementary schools on how to communicate effectively, how to have better relationships, or how to live authentically. Imagine if valuable life lessons could be taught to young children to foster better human contribution and connection?

The first component of communication is to *set good intentions* for the relationship. This means the intention to be open and willing to improve the standards of communication with your partner, possibly a mutually agreeable intention to improve communication between the two of you. It is assumed that there is an awareness on both parts that the potential for improvement exists. Setting intention is so powerful, and can be a valuable strategy in other areas of life. Setting intention is mentally and physically preparing to commit to a chosen task or effort by committing all parts of yourself to the successful outcome. The brain and body align to prepare for an intended result. Setting the intention to *not* go to bed angry with your partner results in a combined effort to find ways to reach a more desirable state before going to sleep. How about a conversation, a game, sex, tv, yoga, bath time, or meditation, to name a few examples.

The second component of communication is to *verbalize* to your partner what is specifically bothering you and that it needs to be addressed immediately. It is recommended to verbalize only one specific topic or issue at a time, to keep on point, and maintain clarity for each other. Often people will sweep things under the carpet like I described in my personal story. This means the small annoyances or concerns tend to be ignored or thought to be not important, until the mound under the carpet becomes the elephant in the room and can no longer be overlooked. It is better to verbalize things that cause known changes to your physiology, because that is your indication that it has disrupted your value system or challenged your beliefs past the point of toleration. It is always worth communicating those little things with your partner to avoid creating a mountain out of a mole hill, as the saying goes.

The third component of communication involves *listening* to your partner; that is, actively listening. This means there is a deeper layer of listening to what they are saying, not planning out what you are going to say next. Have you ever gone to a social event, been introduced to someone and wham, in 10 seconds you have forgotten their name? Often it is because you are not fully present, not actively listening, or engaged in what the other person is saying. You may have heard someone speak, but been guilty of not actually listening? Deeper listening requires practice, and when you are genuinely interested in another person, you are more likely to actively lean in and register what they are saying, in terms of words, intent, and even what is *not* said out loud.

As a life coach, this is one of the most important spaces to hold for a client. Often times I have been told by clients that I am the only one that truly listens to them. Poor listening skills is not shorthand for not caring; the reality is that some people have not mastered the art of deep listening nor had the opportunity to model from someone who does listen intently. A strong component of deep listening is to *not talk*. You know the saying "two ears, one mouth?" There is an obvious reason for that. Another point in the skill of artful listening is to position your body close enough to your partner to be intimate; that means somewhere between across the room and in each other's personal space. When you want to discuss matters of the heart, or points of contention, it is vital to hold the space for each other respectfully. Positioning your body in a positive, receptive way during a conversation can greatly improve the quality of engagement.

The last point I want to stress about good listening skills is to acknowledge and engage with your partner while you converse. This might be a nod of the head, a leaning in position, a soft verbal acknowledgement or just a smile. This encourages your partner to continue to share their story with a captive audience, meaning someone who cares.

The fourth component in the strategy of communication is *reciprocation,* which means sharing the space and respecting the person who has the microphone at the time. It is about taking turns; one person listens intently and attentively, while waiting patiently for their air time. This is a really important step, because there are some other factors that are at play. Reciprocation is a natural flow from listening because first you must actively listen to what your partner says, then you effectively repeat back what they said in a sentence or two to be sure that you understood what you heard. You are looking for clarity so that you can speak to the subject without jumping to conclusions or missing the mark completely.

This process of back-and-forth builds connection because each person feels they are being heard. Reciprocation is a polite exchange of information and ideas in the art of communication. Is the subject matter always rainbows and popsicles? Of course not. Sometimes the subject matter is difficult and emotional, making it more challenging to get through the conversation with the best execution of your intentional communication strategies. But the practice of reciprocation alone can help ward off the tendency to want to "over-talk" your partner. Interrupting and over-talking is an example of needing to be heard, controlling a situation, and it expresses your lack of concern about your partner's point of view. The final step of *honoring* your partner's words makes any conversation sacred and protected. Honor can sometimes present itself when a couple agrees to disagree, such as when a conversation escalates into a heated argument. It is more desirable to acknowledge and appreciate differing perspectives without personal attacks on character or personally held beliefs. We should always seek to understand first.

Rona, a 42-year-old police officer, had a strained marriage. In part, this was due to the fact that her work culture was very private and she could not share much of her day with her husband. They had been married for eleven years, but the past year, they really didn't talk much. They shared less about what took up most of their day, and in the evenings they devoted all their time and attention to their 8-year-old son. Often one of them would drive their son to soccer practice while the other one cooked dinner. Nights were busy and when their son went to sleep, both parents would grab a glass of wine to relax. Except they each went in their own direction—either catching up on their work for the next day, or doing something passive like surfing the net or watching tv. She did recognize that both of their careers were stressful, and the workload seemed insurmountable at times. Both were high achievers. This was one of the characteristics that attracted them to each other when they met in college.

Rona worked hard in the first ten years of her marriage to attain top ranks in the force. She also managed to have a pregnancy, then attempted to balance the demands of motherhood and the rank of sergeant at the station. She said that she and her husband were just managing their days, but the stress was high and their communication was often short, abrupt, and superficial. Not that discussing current affairs, traffic patterns, or the weather needs to be omitted, but what was missing for Rona and so many others in her situation was the substance, the deep, soulful connection she once had with her partner. As time passed, Rona admitted that they began to *run the business* of marriage, but never really talked about anything interesting. They rarely talked about their feelings or the goals they had for their family.

During our sessions, we focused on the components of communication and how they applied to Rona's relationship. We worked through each of the components: intention, verbalizing, listening, reciprocation, and honoring, as I articulated earlier in this chapter. In Rona's case her *intention* was to improve the communication with her husband, and more specifically, to make a conscious effort to ask better questions to elicit answers that went beyond superficial. After just one session, Rona went back to her husband and *verbalized* her concern that they needed to connect through daily conversation because she felt distanced from him.

Through all the points of active listening and reciprocation she had practiced with me, she had a positive result with her first attempt to communicate with her husband.

He was very receptive to her concerns because her delivery was so planned. There was no reason to feel defensive or attacked in any way, because Rona had first identified how they could work together to improve communication. They shared that intention, therefore the implementation of the other components fell into place and created a more workable solution to having better conversations and greater connection. They have room to grow in their relationship by continuing to apply the components of the art of communication, but have made great strides in learning how to listen to each other. As a side note, the work we have done together has mapped over to Rona's work life, and fostered better communication with her staff and superiors.

How could you improve communication with someone you know? How could you enhance your relationship in some way with that person? Write down what your intention is for having a conversation with this person. What is the specific topic you wish to address? This would be what you verbalize to the person. Imagine yourself doing this, say it out loud, hear what that sounds like. Get comfortable saying it so that you can begin to have a conversation with this person in a relaxed and controlled manner. The next step is to actively listen to what that person's response is, then reciprocate in such a way that honors that person, that you heard what they said, and most importantly, that it resonated with you. These steps would be repeated in a normal conversation and with practice and time, communication can be improved and a deeper level of connection can result.

# CHAPTER 9

## Knowledge - Own it!

"When we know better, we do better!" MAYA ANGELOU

Knowledge is so powerful, we should always seek to understand and learn new things all the time. Knowing can be a noun in the sense of this process, as in having a "knowing" of the place you have arrived to in terms of your relationship. When you have worked through all the previous stages in the 8 Progressive Steps, you will get to this innate state of knowing where you stand, as well as what you won't stand *for* anymore.

As I mentioned in previous chapters, this process could take months or years to fully work through. There is no timeline or recommended formula for how long each of the 8 Progressive Steps will take; it depends on the individuals, how partners work together, and all their unique relationship characteristics. Outcomes are dependent on those variables, plus with all the internal work being done, the whole relationship experiences a shift and a progression. This takes time and energy to sort through.

At this stage in the process, I would like for you to start by owning *where you are now*. What is the present state of knowing like for you? Step fully into the uncomfortable-ness of your current situation. When you do this, you align with your values, you focus energy on what is important to you. Any misalignment of values, which become visible as you notice discomfort, will give hints on what needs to be adjusted. You can only make a decision about what is best for you growing forward if your head, heart, and gut are aligned. When this happens, you can make decisions and act from a place of authenticity. This stage requires you to listen to yourself, to trust your inner voice, ask yourself resourceful questions.

Envision the person you dream about being, hold tight to your values, and act with the noblest of intentions. Rise above the obstacles, keep your eye on the goal, embrace vul-nerability and be courageous. Ask for help, cry when you need to–but be willing to risk making a decision once you come to this place of knowing. Embrace it.

I had worked with Georgia for three years during her on-again, off-again relationship. Her husband Kent had had an affair with their neighbor, and despite her anger and desire to divorce, something kept holding her back from following through. She had been married for 28 years by that time, and couldn't even imagine a life without her husband. They had two kids in high school and one still in elementary school. She felt as if she had no choice but to stay–for the kids, of course. She was so angry that her husband had betrayed the family, had poisoned their love, and yet he continued to live in the same house. Georgia was miserable for the first year and a half after the discovery, and she gained over 40 pounds, as she was engaged in emotional eating to try and make herself feel better. The truth was she was feeling worse as time went by, because she was masking the reality of her feelings about her situation, and not having the energy and confidence to make more constructive changes for herself. She was completely misaligned with her values and therefore didn't "know" what she was going to do, and that was what kept her stuck. This was going to be a layered approach to remove barriers to her knowing. We spent most of our time together at first keeping her physical body fit with proper nutrition, so that she could then work on her emotional health and come to terms with the reality of her relationship status.

We spent many sessions creating deeper awareness about the affair, acknowledging how she felt about it, and how that impacted her and the family. By breaking down the emotional trauma to the single event of her husband cheating, we were able to arrive at the drivers that caused her specific upset.

We were able to determine that Georgia's sadness predominantly came from the place of feeling *unworthy*. She believed that she was never pretty enough, a belief she carried throughout childhood. Her husband's affair further cemented that belief, because he "chose someone prettier." She was reinforcing her belief with false information, however it was very real, especially in her unconscious mind. Georgia was angry because she had invested 28 years with this man and she felt completely disrespected by his behavior and his choices.

Over the period of a year, Georgia did a lot of personal discovery work to learn more about who she was, what was important to her, and in turn she created a vision of how her life should be. We worked through the 8 Straight Steps together, and Georgia made her major turning point at this stage–arriving at her 'knowing' that she deserved better. She met her authentic self! She told me in a subsequent session that she was leaving her husband because she could no longer look at her husband the same way. She deserved to be happy, treated respectfully, and loved unconditionally. Most importantly, she wanted to set a good example for her kids. Georgia is now living on her own in the family home with her three kids, and the ex-husband resides with the neighbor with whom he had the affair.

Maybe, you are reading this thinking to yourself "this is like my situation!" You could be at this stage now, or still seeking that alignment between your head, heart, and gut that represents the "knowing." This is a stage you arrive at when you know you can *no longer* continue to live in your current situation. You are standing in your authenticity, so own it! Despite the difficulty in arriving at a decision, you accept that something must change and you are willing to take that step.

Who are you now? How do you know that you are being authentic? What aren't you willing to compromise? What needs to change? And why? Write down the answers to these questions and really let them resonate within, so you can start to do better, because you now *know* better.

# CHAPTER 10

## Conversation - Have It!

"A conversation is so much more than words; a conversation is eyes, smiles, silences between the words." ANNIKA THOR

Conversations are always taking place throughout your journey and in this process of growing forward, but *the conversation* at this stage is the *key* conversation. This is the stage where your decision to make a change is announced out loud to your partner. Once you have stood in your place of 'knowing' and you are clear about what needs to happen for you to move forward in life and in your relationship, you must have a direct conversation with your partner.

The reason I created the 8 Progressive Step process is to prevent a partner from being wholly blindsided by your desire to change your relationship status, or even its default norms. The whole intention behind this book is to establish a framework for change, growth, and possibility. It is a useful guide on what to do in the meantime, too, if you are not prepared to face the finality of separation.

I am not saying that your spouse may still not be surprised by your reaction, because many times there is no indication things are "that" bad, or one partner may have some denial about what they are being told, or perhaps they have experienced some relationship flare-ups that settled back into a comfortable status quo.

The conversation may be had in a private setting or in the presence of a marriage counselor, mediator, or similar professional. This type of direct conversation is more like an announcement, as it has the element of completion attached to it. This represents the end of the line for the marriage, that last train to Clarksville, the final countdown. This conversation generally is indicative of having passed the point of no return–because after arriving at a place of owning your dissatisfaction with your situation, you just "know" that there is nothing that can be done to salvage the relationship.

Yolanda, a super energetic and funny client of mine, did some coaching with me recently. She came to the session saying things like, "I am too old for this shit, my husband is fat and lazy, and I am fit and feeling fabulous. After 32 years, I cannot tolerate another with him." It was such a loaded statement that I asked her to sit down and elaborate a little on her situation. In short, she was in her "knowing" state already– we hadn't had any opportunity to travel the previous 5 steps together. She was authentically, effectively, practicing this out loud on me before she announced it to her husband.

I calibrated her body language and her words, and was then convinced that she had indeed worked through my process however unconsciously over the past 8 years on her own, and she was clearly ready to take action. She is currently loving her life and feels like she's 29 all over again, enjoying her friends and her grown children. She is good friends with her husband now, I think in part because she is such a ray of light, and her sense of humor makes it easy to be amicable and friendly. She is enjoying the peace inside her, and the sense of freedom she has achieved, all for making a decision–the avoidance of which had weighed her down for so long.

The step of having the "announcement" conversation is a little like jumping off a high diving board, or going on a really crazy roller coaster loop. As with all those life thrills, this conversation could make you a little sick or shaky to think about, or at times it might have you on edge, and it has a similar outcome of euphoria, of release, of pride in yourself, of feelings of completion. Some clients have told me that they felt physically lighter, as if a literal weight was lifted off their shoulders. Others have felt a subtler sensation, like openness in their chest or a warmth in their stomach. While some experience a newfound clarity in their head, the most common theme is *space*: heart space, open chakras, flow, possibility. I know that for me, it was a relief to announce what I had protected inside for so long.

If you are ready for "the conversation" you may experience butterflies in your stomach, which could be simply nerves, but my suggestion is that it is anticipation, excitement, because you know that the outcome is going to be better.

You deserve to be the best version of yourself. Listen to yourself, get grounded and align your head, heart, and gut. Trust every aspect of your journey to this moment. You have done the work to ensure you are acting in total integrity and positive intention for you, your partner, and your family. Have the conversation you have been putting off for way too long. Your authentic life is worth every moment of it. This book supports the growth of individuals by assisting them through navigating some complex challenges in life and relationships, in order to realize the possibilities that exist for each of them and their family. I am so glad you are with me so far; there is one more essential step to embrace as you grow forward.

# CHAPTER 11

## Growing Forward - Move It!

"You will either step forward into growth or you will step backward into safety." ABRAHAM MASLOW

You have arrived at the final stage of the 8 Progressive Step process, and it represents completion. All the foundational and transitional work has been done, and you are now able to resume planning for your future. As I mentioned in the earlier action step, there is a connotation of movement in a forward direction as opposed to being complacent or stuck. This action step encompasses the entire relationship system growing forward, not just yourself but your partner, your family, other shared relationships, etc. Family takes on a new definition, your relationship takes on a new form, and your outlook on the future is one of "I" with the inclusion of those in your circle you are growing with, including your once partner.

This action step is fluid and gathers with it on your journey the wisdom and know-how to not just survive but thrive. This is also a point of celebration because you made a decision to step up to your identity, embracing your authenticity. You have a vision of how you would like to live your life and why it is important to you. This place of "being" is one of higher self, and the journey or process may have taken a long time, perhaps had a few speed bumps along the way. Once again, it's the importance of holding positive intention for yourself and others, especially your partner.

This step may be logistical in the sense of moving into your own space, providing for yourself financially, taking on more personal responsibilities. Perhaps this could mean a leap of faith that you have been holding back on because you felt you didn't have the support to invest in it. Whatever actions you need to take to grow into your best self, write them down, review them regularly, introduce new plans, but take your time and enjoy the process. We all remember the outcome in the story of the tortoise and the hare; there is no hurry, action does not need to be taken in haste.

Positive change takes time to nurture so be patient with the process of growing forward. That is why the 8 Progressive Steps are designed to be a strategic process to help people take action in their relationship.

I worked through each one of these 8 Progressive Steps recently with a 45-year-old client, Sandra. She had coaching sessions once per week for just over six months and her progress was undeniably quick considering her complex situation. She had been married to Steve for two years. It was her second marriage. The initial reason she gave for booking a session with me was that she needed to figure out *why* she decided to marry a second time. Given her circumstances—her first husband had died suddenly of a heart attack only a year earlier–she termed this second marriage as a rebound relationship. She felt she had made a mistake by marrying Steve for the wrong reasons, and worse yet, she couldn't articulate what those reasons were at all. It was unsettling for her to confront all of this.

What Sandra was able to determine for herself was that she was sad to have lost the love of her life so unexpectedly, and admittedly she was lonely and afraid during that time. She was comforted by Steve, a family friend–who soon grew to be a romantic interest–and next thing she knew, she was getting married. Fast-forward two years, and she was sitting in my office telling me, "I was never in love with Steve. I need time to be on my own, and wish to focus on my daughter and my new grandbaby." She empathetically continued, "I do not want to hurt Steve, but know there is no future for us as a married couple, and it is not what I want." In this scenario, our work together moved quickly through the strategies. Confirming her inner work was done, she moved resolutely to Step 7, which was having the conversation with Steve. To Sandra's relief and surprise, he felt the same. He believed their friendship could continue and that marriage may have been a radical and unnecessary step for both of them in that time of grief.

Sandra began to envision the life she wanted, and was willing to work with Steve to take some action steps to grow forward individually and together as friends. She wanted to put her effort and energy into the new role of Grandma, and Steve was excited to be a part of that family in some fashion. She was so much happier in the company of Steve now, because they had a genuine connection as friends, and no more tension from pretending the relationship was working, or avoiding true feelings. They finalized their divorce after Sandra moved in with her daughter to take care of her granddaughter. Sandra and Steve remain good friends and continue to be supportive of each other's personal journeys in life and love.

Action that is purposeful and supports the growth of *both* people in a relationship should always be a priority. If you have taken action toward your plan, and are currently in this phase of exiting a relationship, I hope this book supports you and confirms your experience as you continue to execute your personal plan for future growth. Growing forward yourself, taking opportunities to learn more, and do more, enables you to continue to work on yourself and even nurture a supportive and encouraging friendship with your ex-partner.

Positive intention in all regards helps everyone to stay on the diligent path of cooperation. Inject respect and a little love into the recipe of communication and decision-making going forward. Perhaps your goal is to set a good example for your kids, or maybe it is time to honor yourself and love yourself enough to bring full awareness and emotional integrity into your life. Step forward!

# CHAPTER 12

## The Obstacles

"Obstacles don't have to stop you. If you run into a wall, don't turn around and give up. Figure out how to climb it, go through it, or work around it." MICHAEL JORDAN

I believe I mentioned earlier that the 8 Progressive Steps are not all about rainbows and popsicles. The truth is, it *is* hard work, and you will absolutely come up against some obstacles. Maybe at least one at every single step! That's where my coaching guidance and this book can help you the most. Perhaps you are currently experiencing some obstacles or speed bumps in your relationship?

I should also mention that there are some relationship scenarios in which this process is not appropriate—or at least not the most effective way to achieve your ideal result. For example, I suggest seeking a different source for advice or professional help if you are in an abusive relationship, or there is some form of addiction at play in your relationship. Elements of those situations and therapeutic needs of one or both partners make it more complicated to get through the entire process.

I should also stress that any journey of this magnitude should *not* be done entirely alone. We are human and we need support, therefore the process I offer in this book is also most effective when you are working through the steps in conjunction with coaching. I have witnessed the journeys of many people who started in places very similar to where you are right now. This might be a good time to look at the 8 Progressive Step Strategy I offer through my website www.straightupcoaching.com.

There are certain steps in the process that may hold especially significant value in your current relationship. If your purpose is to grow separate from your partner, then the process is best followed from beginning to end. You may experience getting stuck on a step because your partner is not on board with your decision. You may experience full derailment when your spouse hires a lawyer to make your life miserable and erode your happy process.

Wherever you are now, this process can help you overcome the difficult situations you may be in, and recognize that no situation is permanent. Even if you have conjured up a whole story in your head that seems hard to manage, then this process will support your personal growth. In all of the client examples I have shared, these people have moved through this process toward an amicable resolution with me coaching them at each step. You too can have a happy ending, which in this case is comprised of a new beginning. There is hope for you and the person with whom you once fell in love and planned a forever together. Forever

is here and now–and you are co-creating a new definition of family and friendship that fosters respect and love
while supporting each other's quest to be the best version
of yourselves. How refreshing to know that we can create
our own version of "happily ever after," even post-divorce.
How refreshing not to be limited by our unwillingness to
admit our relationships no longer fit, without need for
blame, instead focusing on the joy-affirming reasons for
everyone involved.

Relationships can be messy sometimes and should you sail
through the first three steps yourself, you may then hit an
obstacle in the form of a past belief. Beliefs create speed-
bumps. They are the conclusions about life that we started
building in our childhood through our unique influences
and experiences, and they are hard to shake. It is possible that a belief can freeze your progress, and you may not
recognize or know how to move through it. This is where
coaching around personal beliefs and values is priceless,
because beliefs can be hidden to the believer, and because
they can also be changed. Working with me on the process
avoids unnecessary time moving through the steps, and
avoidance of being stranded in one stage.

Using the 8 Progressive Steps, especially combined with an
investment in personal coaching, can save you thousands of
dollars in unnecessary legal fees. Divorce can leave people
feeling bitter towards each other and even more bitter
towards the lawyers, who usually fuel the animosity and
take a significant cut of the pie, then disappear from your

lives. Just last month one of my divorced clients said she wished she had my 8 Progressive Steps when she decided to separate from her husband. They did what they thought they should, what they believed people always do, hire a lawyer, who structures asset division taking care of all the paperwork and formalities. As a result, she spent $34,000 to complete the entire process–and they do not have a friendship as a result.

Wouldn't it be more desirable to save that kind of money to invest back into your separate futures, and protect the assets that you and your partner accumulated in your years together? Wouldn't it seem healthy to carry forth an amicable friendship from the roots of your shared past? This could make a tremendous difference toward your own emotional wellbeing and that of your entire circle of influence, especially any kids, whether they live at home or have fled the nest. This process saves money, you learn to know yourself and communicate your needs and perspectives on a whole new level, and amicably work through the separation. The process as outlined in this book preserves relationships and sets a better example for younger generations to follow while offering a whole new world of possibilities to those brave enough to undertake the journey.

# CONCLUSION

"I've learned that people will forget what you said, people will forget what you did, but people will never forget how you made them feel." MAYA ANGELOU

Rachel's story was the first example in this book of a woman feeling like the life was being sucked out of her every single day. She felt she had no choice but to stay in her situation and continue to feel stuck. My personal story, and many of the client stories I shared with you in these pages, carried the weight of burden, and demonstrable tension that mostly came about as a result of poor communication and evasion of the truth. The highlight of the struggle phase is to ask yourself "What is this costing you? What will happen if you continue to endure the emotional pain?"

I'm promising the possibility of a brighter future, to free oneself from the ties that bind whatever that may represent for someone. You don't have to be in a relationship that you are unhappy in, you do have a choice to create something better. There are no universal rules about how to marry, or cohabitate; and there are no rules on how to divorce. However, there is a process on how to separate in an amicable way that is mutually beneficial. That process is in this book and outlined in Chapters 4-11.

The process, 8 Progressive Steps, was inspired by coaching and NLP principles I have used with clients for several years. I have had great success with these principles and would like to reach out to people who are struggling in their current relationships. I would like to see a collective consciousness evolve about the way we end relationships. About how we look at divorce and the expectations we put on the concept of marriage. I want people to realize it is possible to be friends after a separation and that it is possible to grow forward with love and respect for each other. I want to share a conversation my husband and I shared while I was in Hawaii writing this book. Just for the record, I did not intend to write "Growing Your Separate Ways" when I set out to write my book. I feel as if the messages in this book needed to be shared and I was being called upon.

Getting back to the conversation with my husband while I was writing my book... We had already been living apart for a short time and still had not completed any sort of formal separation agreement. I realized my book was taking on a twist that incorporated more of "our story" and I felt out of respect, I should ask him if he was ok with me sharing some details about our journey together. Here is what he texted back... "I understand the value in sharing to help others, it's part of what I often offered as how we could have been so good together. Although our learnings came from decades shared together, your perspective will be from your lens and from your heart, which is loving and is the place I fell in love with. It is a beautiful love story and represents what is possible and that is what I'm all about. I celebrate with joy and happiness for all you are and how you shared and gave to me. Always and forever, D." When I read this, I had tears in my eyes and warmth in my heart.

My response: "Having written this book, reflecting.... knowing that we still 'love' each other is special. I don't know what the future looks like but I do have a vision about how our new family dynamics will be. I want you to know that I support you in life and love and whatever you decide to do or whoever you decide to be with is ok with me. But I want you to know that I have never ruled out that even though our paths are growing separate ways, they may come together again at some point in our journey. Do not stop living in the meantime."

I share this conversation as an example of what is possible for you. When you share some of the best parts of yourself, and experience some of life's most amazing memories together, why would you want anything other than love and friendship growing forward?

We talked about first having the AWARENESS - *embrace it* - that you need to be proactive in your efforts to preserve your relationship. The next step is VISUALIZATION - *see it* - imagining a more desirable place to be or way to be. When you can CLARIFY - *understand it* - specific challenges in the relationship it becomes easier to break them down to more manageable bits. We take all the specific information into consideration and take ACTION - *plan it* - that will inevitably land you a different, more desirable outcome. Action plans are designed for every specific scenario or characteristic; this stage can take longer in the process if there are several issues to deal with. The next step is COMMUNICATION - *say it* - this will not be successful unless all of the previous steps have been sorted through.

Communication is one of the most important steps in the process and a key component to any healthy relationship. Time is set aside for *verbalizing, listening, reciprocating,* and *honoring,* in this sequence. This, too, can be repeated as many times as necessary to master the art of being a good communicator. After this stage, the next, most natural step is arriving at a place of authenticity, KNOWLEDGE - *own it* - how you feel without a doubt. This leads to having the CONVERSATION - *have it* - about the decision to separate. The action that must take place to successfully embrace a new way of being - GROWING FORWARD - *move it* - along the journey ahead, as individuals.

My wish for you is that you embrace this book and the 8 Progressive Steps as a supportive tool to hold onto in your journey. I want to continue to provide inspiration to people to pursue the best versions of themselves and to trust their inner voice and, above all, believe that anything is possible if you want it badly enough.

"Your time is limited, so don't waste it living someone else's life. Don't be trapped by dogma—which is living with the results of other people's thinking. Don't let the noise of others' opinions drown out your own inner voice. And most important, have the courage to follow your heart and intuition." **STEVE JOBS**

The theme of intention, awareness, communication, and respect are key components of each of the eight steps in this process. These are important values that are also present in a healthy relationship—with anyone else, and indeed with yourself. The point I want to highlight is the process of separating can be done, with love and positive intentions, just as you probably approached all the changes you created in your lives when you were getting married. It might not be perfect, it might be messy at times, and for sure there is always something to learn. If there are kids involved, it is important to remember that you are still their parents, and you are *all* creating a new definition of family.

Let's embrace a new collective consciousness now and for our future generations. One that does not paint divorce as dark and painful, and which alternatively presents marriage as a union of best intentions. Relationships that foster love and respect throughout the journey, even when people grow their separate ways.

# EPILOGUE

## One year later....

Reflecting on this past year after growing our separate ways, feels like it was the right thing for us to do at the right time. Each of us has embarked on our own journeys of healing and personal growth in a way that supports our unique needs. While we have not spent much time together, we remain respectful of each other and lovingly support the care and support of our teenage kids. Staying kind throughout the process is a necessity; choosing love instead of anger, fear or frustration is what pulls one in the right direction. Having good intentions creates good vibrations. I am enjoying the simplicity of life, with more emphasis on the present, not sweating small things and appreciating everyone and everything that comes into my circle. I have found a place of peace, thanks to the process outlined in my book.

# Acknowledgements

I want to celebrate the completion of this book by acknowledging all the teachers, trainers, and facilitators who contributed to my knowledge and skillset over the years.

To all my valued clients—past and present—who have invested in themselves, in turn allowing me to travel on their journey towards optimal physical, mental, and spiritual health.

I want to thank ALL the friends throughout my lifetime for their support and encouragement, especially the ones that remain in my inner circle.

I am grateful for my parents who provided me with the best childhood memories, instilling a belief that I could do anything I put my mind to.

To all other family, in-laws included, for being there through thick or thin.

A special thank you to Derrick for always believing in my aspirations, trusting my crazy decisions and being a supportive, loving, involved Dad.

Most importantly, I want to acknowledge our children, Chelsea and Jaden, for becoming genuine, authentic, compassionate, loving young adults; you make us proud!

# About The Author

Leah has a full, abundant life; always a delicate juggling of work-life balance. Her motto is 'work hard, play harder.' Family is most important; however, she has a relentless ambition to make a global impact in the area of self-development, taking into consideration physical and mental well-being. Building awareness, getting unstuck, creating a vision, taking action, embracing authenticity, celebrating the little things and loving life are entwined in her coaching strategies.

Leah began her career as a personal fitness trainer over 27 years ago. After spending many years in management of large fitness chains, she pursued her entrepreneurial goal of owning her own health club. After twelve successful years as a CEO and thousands of client sessions later, Leah began to realize that there was something missing in the process of physical transformation. That capacity for human potentiality was hidden within the client, and had more to do with who they believed themselves to be and what their model of the world was.

Leah sold her business to pursue higher learning about NLP and psychology, in an effort to discover how to create lasting change for a client. A "game changer" attitude taking on all challenges, overcoming obstacles, working through the weeds to eventually smell the flowers. Lasting change, happy lives, peace, joy, love. After all, isn't that what we are all searching for under some superficial statement like.... "I just need to lose weight and then..." or "If I could only make more money I could..." and "When my kids grow up I will get...." Leah addresses these excuses to uncover the real motivation behind the words.

Leah is a master in the field of human potentiality and transformation supported by thousands of client testimonials of success. She is passionate about helping people get 'unstuck' and create visions about who they want to *be*, what they want to *do*, and what they will *have* as a result of their consistent action and transformed beliefs.

difference press

Difference Press offers entrepreneurs, including life coaches, healers, consultants, and community leaders, a comprehensive solution to get their books written, published, and promoted. A boutique-style alternative to self-publishing, Difference Press boasts a fair and easy-to-understand profit structure, low-priced author copies, and author-friendly contract terms. Its founder, Dr. Angela Lauria, has been bringing to life the literary ventures of hundreds of authors-in-transformation since 1994.

---

### LET'S MAKE A DIFFERENCE WITH YOUR BOOK

You've seen other people make a difference with a book. Now it's your turn. If you are ready to stop watching and start taking massive action, reach out.

"Yes, I'm ready!"

In a market where hundreds of thousands books are published every year and are never heard from again, all participants of The Author Incubator have bestsellers that are actively changing lives and making a difference.

In two years we've created over 134 bestselling books in a row, 90% from first-time authors. We do this by selecting the highest quality and highest potential applicants for our future programs.

Our program doesn't just teach you how to write a book—our team of coaches, developmental editors, copy editors, art directors, and marketing experts incubate you from book idea to published bestseller, ensuring that the book you create can actually make a difference in the world. Then we give you the training you need to use your book to make the difference you want to make in the world, or to create a business out of serving your readers. If you have life-or world-changing ideas or services, a servant's heart, and the willingness to do what it REALLY takes to make a difference in the world with your book, go to http://theauthorincubator.com/apply/ to complete an application for the program today.

*Clarity Alchemy: When Success Is Your Only Option*

by Ann Bolender

*Cracking the Code: A Practical Guide to Getting You Hired*

by Molly Mapes

*Divorce to Divine: Becoming the Fabulous Person You Were Intended to Be*

by Cynthia Claire

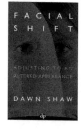

*Facial Shift: Adjusting to an Altered Appearance*

by Dawn Shaw

*Finding Clarity: Design a Business You Love and Simplify Your Marketing*

by Amanda H. Young

*Flourish: Have It All Without Losing Yourself*

by Dr. Rachel Talton

*Marketing To Serve: The Entrepreneur's Guide to Marketing to Your Ideal Client and Making Money with Heart and Authenticity*

by Cassie Parks

*NEXT: How to Start a Successful Business That's Right for You and Your Family*

by Caroline Greene

Pain Free: How I
Released 43 Years
of Chronic Pain

by Dottie DuParcé
(Author), John F.
Barnes (Foreword)

Secret Bad Girl:
A Sexual Trauma
Memoir and
Resolution Guide

by Rachael
Maddox

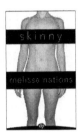

Skinny: The Teen
Girl's Guide to
Making Choices,
Getting the Thin
Body You Want,
and Having the
Confidence You've
Always Dreamed Of

by Melissa Nations

The Aging Boomers:
Answers to Critical
Questions for You,
Your Parents and
Loved Ones

by Frank M. Samson

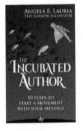

The Incubated
Author: 10 Steps to
Start a Movement
with Your Message

by Angela Lauria

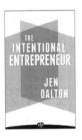

The Intentional
Entrepreneur: How
to Be a Noisebreaker,
Not a Noisemaker

by Jen Dalton
(Author), Jeanine
Warisse Turner
(Foreword)

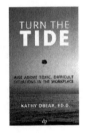

The Paws Principle:
Front Desk
Conversion Secrets
for the Vet Industry

by Scott Baker

Turn the Tide:
Rise Above Toxic,
Difficult Situations
in the Workplace

by Kathy Obear

# Thank You For Reading My Book!

If something touched you in this book or you were inspired in some way, please share with me, I would love to hear about it. Email me at straightupcoaching@gmail.com

I would love to have you join my "tribe" and have access to free blogs, videos, and daily motivational quotes by visiting www.straightupcoaching.com.

In appreciation of your support, if you read the book and thought that the "8 Progressive Steps" may help you in your situation, I would like to extend an offer to you for a one-hour strategy session by phone. The potential to design your own outcome is possible. I look forward to walking the journey alongside you.

Printed in Great Britain
by Amazon

29570913R00071